M000302718

The Golem, How He Came into the World

German Film Classics

Also in the Series

Fitzcarraldo, by Lutz Koepnick
Phoenix, by Brad Prager
The White Ribbon, by Fatima Naqvi
Wings of Desire, by Christian Rogowski

THE GOLEM, HOW HE CAME INTO THE WORLD

MAYA BARZILAI

CAMDEN HOUSE

First published 2020 by Camden House

Camden House is an imprint of Boydell & Brewer Inc.
668 Mt. Hope Avenue, Rochester, NY 14620, USA
www.camden-house.com
and of Boydell & Brewer Limited
PO Box 9, Woodbridge, Suffolk IP12 3DF, UK
www.boydellandbrewer.com

ISBN-13: 978-1-64014-030-1
ISBN-10: 1-64014-030-1

Cover image: The golem runs amok, setting Rabbi Loew's house on fire. Screen shot from *Der Golem, wie er in die Welt kam.*

Library of Congress Cataloging-in-Publication Data

CIP data applied for.

This publication is printed on acid-free paper.
Printed in the United States of America.

Publication of this book was supported by a grant from the German Film Institute (GFI) of the University of Michigan Department of Germanic Languages & Literatures.

CONTENTS

ACKNOWLEDGMENTS

The initial research for this book was generously supported by the Berlin Program for Advanced German and European Studies. The Deutsche Kinemathek Museum für Film und Fernsehen Berlin, including the film, photo, and personal papers archives, as well as the archive of the Deutsches Filminstitut und Filmmuseum Frankfurt am Main, helped me to access materials pertaining to Paul Wegener and the three golem films. I also benefitted from an NEH summer stipend and a year-long fellowship at the Frankel Institute for Advanced Studies, allowing me to complete the research and writing for my first book, *Golem: Modern Wars and Their Monsters* (2016). I am grateful to Jennifer Hammer at NYU Press for her wise stewardship of that book, and to NYU Press for allowing me to use parts of my chapter "The Face of Destruction: Paul Wegener's World War I Golem Film" as the basis for the current book.

At the University of Michigan, Jonathan Freedman, Deborah Dash Moore, Rafe Neis, Anita Norich, and Jeffrey Veidlinger have lent their supportive eyes and ears, commenting on manuscript drafts and encouraging my golem pursuits. My colleague and editor Johannes von Moltke enthusiastically backed this project, providing invaluable guidance on how to construct a volume devoted to a single film. Gerd Gemünden and the anonymous reviewer of the manuscript offered highly useful feedback and many words of encouragement. I was very fortunate to work with Jim Walker at Camden House: his devotion to the project even during a pandemic was exemplary; his eye for incongruities and his elegant stylistic touch have transformed this manuscript.

Special thanks go to my parents and sister for sustaining me with their love, wise advice, and technical savvy. My kids have raised me to be a better human being and appreciate monsters all the more. Finally, my unending gratitude goes to Russell Bucher, a man of fine analog sensibilities who deeply fathoms my passion for silent film and the printed word.

The golem opens its eyes for the first time.

The Golem, How He Came into the World

Introduction: The Ethics of Animation

Two men prop up a stiff, human-shaped statue, tall and imposing. They point at a round cavity in the middle of its chest. The older man folds up a piece of paper, on which he has written the word *Aemaet* (truth), inserting it into a star-shaped capsule. He then returns to the inanimate figure and places the capsule in the cavity, turning the star. A clay golem comes to life. In this quintessentially cinematic moment, the golem, enacted by Paul Wegener (1874–1948), opens its eyes for the first time. A close-up reveals a down-turned mouth, clay-toned skin, and a sculpted headdress. The eyes move slowly to the left, where Rabbi Loew, the golem's creator, stands gazing in shock. When gestured to move forward, the golem first wobbles in place and then takes a few clumsy steps. Turning and walking in the other direction, it encounters the rabbi's assistant and, with a light shove, knocks him to the ground. Thereby, viewers come to understand that this inordinately strong anthropoid will trample anything that stands in its way.

This scene of the golem's animation occurs thirty minutes into the classic 1920 silent film *Der Golem, wie er in die Welt kam* (*The Golem, How He Came into the World*), co-directed by Wegener and Carl Boese, co-written by Wegener and Henrik Galeen, shot by Karl Freund, and produced by Paul Davidson.[1] The dramatic buildup to the golem's awakening commences with Rabbi Loew's astrological prediction of an impending disaster for the Jewish community. After reading this portent in the night skies, the rabbi begins to mold the golem out of clay, consulting ancient manuals. At the same time, the Emperor of Prague seals his edict of expulsion and sends a messenger, his courtier, to the ghetto to inform the Jews that they must leave within the month. The rabbi proceeds to create the clay golem and uses his strength and stoicism at the imperial court to save the Jews from expulsion. The narrative of the film does not end, however, with the rabbi's success at court. Unbeknownst to him, Miriam, his daughter, conducts an illicit affair with the courtier who delivered the edict. When he discovers the pair, the rabbi's assistant re-animates the golem, who then becomes wild and violent, ultimately murdering Miriam's lover and setting the rabbi's home and the entire ghetto on fire. In this retelling of the famous Prague narrative, the golem runs amok because of the jealousy inspired by the illicit love affair and not because the rabbi forgot to remove the animating device on the Sabbath. In the film's resolution, a Christian child accidentally de-animates the golem.

Having already established himself as a prominent theater actor in Max Reinhardt's Deutsches Theater, Wegener strove, as director and film actor, to distinguish cinema from stage drama and the sensationalist novel.[2] His early film art exhibited what Katharina Loew calls the "technoromantic" approach to cinema. It combined technological expertise with a "romantic commitment to the supersensible."[3] In a pioneering 1917 essay, Wegener stated that "the true poet of the film must be the *camera*," meaning that film technology should dictate the choice of materials to be screened.[4] Starting with his 1913 fairy-tale film, *Der Student von Prag* (*The Student of Prague*), written in collaboration with Hanns Heinz Ewers, Wegener's cinema of the 1910s revolved around fantastical subject matter, emphasizing special effects, such as doubling, and animating magical creatures, including mountain spirits (*Ruebezahl's Wedding*,

1916) and golems.[5] The use of fantastic narrative drawn from German literary lore contributed to the respectability of Wegener's cinematic endeavors, fostering his films' appeal to the educated middle class while maintaining their popularity.[6]

The scene in which the golem first opens its eyes underscores the power of vision, implicitly alerting viewers to their own role as consumers of the nascent cinematic medium: contemporary viewers sat in the movie theater like stiff golems, unmoving, their eyes intensely activated. A similar scene takes place in Robert Wiene's groundbreaking *Das Cabinet des Dr. Caligari* (*The Cabinet of Dr. Caligari*), which premiered earlier in 1920. In a fairground setting, the mysterious character of Dr. Caligari wakes the somnambulist Cesare from a lifetime of slumber, through the touch of his wand. When Cesare awakens, a close-up shot shows Dr. Caligari peering at him. Cesare blinks his eyes for quite a while before opening them wide, staring in an ominous manner. As in *The Golem, How He Came into the World*, Wiene's film postpones the moment of animation—or "act of creation" in the words of Anton Kaes—toying with the audience's anticipation.[7] The result of this awakening or animation is a new form of vision, both in Cesare's newfound eyesight and the somnambulist's ability to "look" into the past and the future.

In addition to its affinities with *The Cabinet of Dr. Caligari*, *The Golem, How He Came into the World* exhibits the Weimar-era preoccupation with artificial creation, which included films such as the six-part *Homunculus* (Otto Rippert, 1916–17), starring a laboratory-created man with superhuman powers, and the famous *Metropolis* (Fritz Lang, 1927), featuring a human machine, the robotic Maria. In Wegener's three golem films, however, magical formulas, rather than scientific experiments, bring to life a clay monster. Emerging from the bowels of the earth and molded in a cave-like laboratory, Wegener's golem bore a metonymic association with the clay of World War I trenches, and was not only a robot or automaton.

The Golem, How He Came into the World, Wegener's most famous silent film, was the third film in which he enacted the clay anthropoid. In the first adaptation, *Der Golem* (*The Golem*, 1914/15), Wegener played a clay monster animated in present-day Germany in order to guard the daughter of a Jewish antiques dealer and prevent her romance with the local baron. In this early film, Wegener and his co-writer Henrik Galeen imagined the golem as a found object, dug up as part of a larger trove. The golem's animation occurs perchance, rather than as part of a well-planned defense strategy. Another romantic drama came out in 1917—*Der Golem und die Tänzerin* (*The Golem and the Dancer*, 1917)—in which Wegener attempts to seduce a variety dancer, played by the Czech actress and dancer Lyda Salmonova, Wegener's off-screen partner at the time.[8] The variety dancer goes to a movie theater and views nothing other than *The Golem* film of 1914/1915. After the screening, she purchases a replica of the golem figure. Viewers see Wegener, in his golem costume, arrive, packaged in a crate, at the dancer's abode, where he pretends to come to life in a menacing and comical flirtation.

While these first two golem films have been lost, with the exception of a few short sequences, stills, and their screenplays, Wegener's third remolding of the clay anthropoid survived through multiple export copies and a recently discovered original negative. Each of the three films constituted a discrete adaptation of the golem narrative, rather than a component in a trilogy. Together they bear witness to the immense potential that Wegener as actor and director found in the golem: this figure and its narrative served him as raw cinematic material that he then molded and remolded, changing its form and function along with the progress of cinema itself. In this respect, the golem served as an index of cinematic history, as contemporaneous critics already noted.[9] It did more than that, though: set in an imagined sixteenth-century Prague, *The Golem, How He Came into the World* was the most politicized and historically attuned of Wegener's golem films. Through a legendary reenactment distanced in its external manifestation from modern-day German, Wegener infused the film with a strong presentist sensibility, informed by his own wartime and postwar experiences.

I interpret the remaining 1920 film within the sociopolitical and biographical context of World War I, showing how it projects a society under great duress—resembling Germany during the war and in its aftermath. In the film, the leader of the Jewish ghetto needs to harness the powers of both magic and technology in order to avoid utter destruction. Cinema becomes a site for reflection on how mass warfare has changed our understanding of the human being and its capacities. Moreover, *The Golem, How He Came into the World* addresses the impact of war and death on human beings through the lens of the Jewish predicament, and not merely through the golem's own attempt to attain a semblance of humanity. It reveals the life-threatening consequences of disowning the (Jewish) minority group, and insists that a non-utilitarian approach to all humans is the foundation of an ethical postwar society.

In October 1914, having completing the shooting of *The Golem*, the almost forty-year-old Wegener volunteered for the *Landsturm*, or reserves, where he served first as a corporal and later as lieutenant.[10] In December of that same year, his battalion came under heavy bombardment near the Yser river, Belgium, and out of his own squad of forty-nine, only Wegener and three others survived. While the newspapers reporting on the 1915 screening of *The Golem* noted Wegener's bravery on the front, private diaries and letters attest to the heavy emotional toll on the actor and his disdain for the war and its devastating effects.[11] *The Golem, How He Came into the World* returns, albeit implicitly, to the trenches of World War I, portraying the Jewish ghetto, in sets designed by renowned modernist architect Hans Poelzig, as a clay battle zone, with tunnels, underground rooms, explosions, and fires. In this film, not only the Jews under siege but also the court and its emperor, representative of the oblivious home front, experience a life-threatening disaster. In the climax of the film, when Rabbi Loew brings the golem to court, the ceiling begins to collapse upon the courtiers after they laugh at a projected scene of wandering Jews. The rabbi then calls upon the golem to hold up the ceiling in exchange for the annulment of the edict ordering the expulsion of the Jews. Reminiscent of the recent war carnage, the partial collapse of the ceiling leads to death and injury in the court, and we see bodies strewn on the floor as the emperor begs Rabbi Loew for his life.

Evoking a battle zone in such scenes, Wegener ultimately used cinema to suggest a path for personal and national recovery, not only to re-create the atrocities of wartime. Through the artificial manipulation of a studio-based mise-en-scène, he sought to uncover the expressive face of both animate and inanimate things. His early "technoromantic" approach to the cinematic medium attained, in this manner, an ethical sense of purpose: the golem's cinematic animation

Chaos and injury at the Prague court.

and de-animation enabled Wegener to explore themes of human fragility and mortality; lack of control over one's existence; and the basic desire for human connection and empathy. The filmmaker's attempt to reveal the spiritual dimension of film coincided with his goal of enacting a golem that emerges, even if briefly, from its obtuse and robotic condition, attaining self-awareness and even a semblance of humanity.

Christian-Jewish relations became the prism through which these postwar concerns unfold in *The Golem, How He Came into the World*. The conflict dramatized in the film also implicitly addressed the worsening status of Jews in Germany during and after World War I. Specifically, the war led to a rise in antisemitism fueled by unfounded accusations of Jewish draft-dodging and political backstabbing, as well as by increased Jewish immigration to Berlin from Eastern Europe. Wegener's 1920 golem film enlists viewers in support of the threatened Jewish community and its leader. It likewise criticizes the emperor's lack of empathy and the frivolous nature of his court, justifying the collapse of the ceiling, which, like a golem of lore, serves due punishment. Peaceable relations between Jews and Christians are restored when the illicit romance between the rabbi's daughter and the Christian aristocrat comes to a violent end and the Jews resume their isolated existence in the ghetto. Unlike the narrative of Jewish assimilation projected in the 1914/1915 golem film, the 1920 film promoted Jewish cultural and territorial separation and independence, hinted at through Zionist symbols and associations.

Critics in Germany and internationally embraced *The Golem, How He Came into the World* upon its release in October of 1920. The "unheard beauty" of its architectural design and cinematography appeared to "surpass its times," entrancing viewers across the globe.[12] Making its way to the United States in the summer of 1921, the film ran for an extended period of sixteen weeks in New York City. It garnered much attention in the English- and Yiddish-language press, leading to numerous golem adaptations across a variety of media: theater, opera, and literature. International circulation ensured its status as a cinematic touchstone, informing subsequent golem and Frankenstein films and comics, from Julien Duviver's 1936 *Le Golem* and James Whale's 1931 *Frankenstein* to James Sturm's 2001 graphic narrative *The Golem's Mighty Swing* and *The Simpsons* 2006 golem spoof. A classic example of Weimar cinema's penchant for artificial creation, fantastic set designs, and implicit social commentary, *The Golem, How He Came into the World* stands out as a unique collaboration among Jewish and non-Jewish artists who brought to life a distinctly postwar golem.

How Wegener Came to the Golem

Wegener's ongoing fascination with the golem narrative attests to the degree to which this tale had become a mainstay of German culture throughout the nineteenth and early twentieth centuries. From the time of Jacob Grimm's 1808 variant of the golem story, attributed to Polish Jews, German authors such as Achim von Arnim began to produce their own literary retellings of this narrative of artificial creation. In Grimm's version, a golem that grows to immense height ultimately falls upon its own creator, a Jew, when the latter attempts to de-animate it, thereby crushing the man to death in its own demise. This sensationalist plot portrayed "Kabbalah as some kind of radical Jewish thaumaturgy."[13] The Prague variant, emerging in the 1830s–1840s, served to counter the Grimm story by attaching the golem to the venerated historical figure of Rabbi Jehudah Loew ben Betzalel, known as the Maharal (our teacher).[14] In contrast to the German narrative of Jewish occult crime and punishment, the Prague version showcases the rabbi's "mastery of the holy word," the name of God, and does not end with his demise.[15] Rather, after the golem runs amok and begins to destroy the ghetto when the rabbi forgets to allow it to rest on the Sabbath, the rabbi manages to de-animate it and restore communal order.

In a 1914 essay entitled "Why I Act in Film" (Warum ich für den Film spiele), Wegener explained that he derived the material for his new film from the "well-known Prague ghetto tale of the golem," adapting it from a cinematic viewpoint while upholding its mythical depths. In this way, Wegener suggested, the film could truly perform the animation of a medieval mystical clay figure.[16] Wegener's three golem films, spanning the years 1914 to 1920, drew from a variety of golem sources, and not only from the Prague tale. As in the German Romantic versions, his Jewish creators use magic rituals, rather than relying on Jewish mystical treatises; at the same time, they are not crushed in the process of de-animation, and, in the 1920 film, Rabbi Loew appears as a powerful master of his art. Gustav Meyrink's novel *Der Golem*, an occult thriller, appeared in 1915 and became a bestseller throughout the war and postwar years. While Wegener's clay giant did not resemble Meyrink's ghostly golem, Hugo Steiner-Prag's illustrations for the novel and Meyrink's anthropomorphic descriptions of the Prague ghetto homes resonated with Wegener's Orientalizing approach to the golem figure and may have provided inspiration for the architecture of the third film.[17]

Finally, in the Jewish Hungarian author Arthur Holitscher's 1908 drama, *The Golem: A Ghetto Legend in Three Acts*, which Wegener read for a lead role at the Deutsches Theater in Berlin, a golem seeks to become more human, to feel joy and love.[18] Holitscher introduced an emotional entanglement to the golem narrative. In Oded Shai's words, "the golem transforms from an obtuse, oppressed, and unreflective thing to a humanoid with feelings, full of yearning for humanness."[19] The rabbi even admits that his plan was to treat the golem like a "dead tool" or a "hammer," but that he gave his creation more life and power than he had intended.[20] The presence of the rabbi's daughter stirs the golem's emotions, but this awakening causes him to recognize "the tragedy of his existence," leading to his frustrated rebellion.[21] Wegener's three films all include a dramatic romance plot, or subplot, in which the golem's desire for the Jewish daughter (or the dancer, in the 1917 film) leads to a horrific chase (1914), a mock animation (1917), and even violent murder (1920). Wegener further enhanced the golem's emotional awakening in these films through scenes set in nature or by evoking a romanticized image of nature with the help of a prop like a rose.

The 1914/1915 *The Golem* is set in modern Germany, in an undefined time period. It opens with the discovery of a treasure trove that includes a gigantic clay figure, subsequently sold to "old Aaron," a local Jewish *Trödler*, or antiques dealer, whose shop contains sculptures of the Buddha, weapons, Oriental lamps, and other curiosities.[22] Aaron, enacted by Wegener's co-writer Henrik Galeen (Heinrich Wiesenberg) accidently discovers how to animate the golem using the star-shaped metal capsule, which, when filled with a piece of parchment containing a magical phrase and placed in the statue's chest, brings it to life.[23] The Prague narrative describes a piece of parchment that, when inscribed with the ineffable name of God and placed in the mouth (also a cavity), animates the golem. While the placement in the mouth does not endow the golem with powers of speech, it locates divine animation in this area, whereas all three silent films draw our attention to the golem's chest, the place of the heart and its emotions of passion and envy. Appropriately, in the first film, the Jewish dealer uses the golem to guard his daughter and attempt to prevent her affair with the local baron. The daughter does not express any emotions towards the golem, as she does in Holitscher's drama, but rather uses her feminine wiles to escape her guard and run away from home to meet her lover. In the chase that ensues, a scene that survived and has been digitally reconstructed, the golem climbs to the top of the tower in pursuit of the couple; following a physical struggle, they manage to throw it off the tower. When Aaron arrives at the scene of this averted tragedy, he reconciles with his daughter, and the baron too joins their embrace at the top of the tower.[24]

The baron throws the de-animated golem off the tower.

Setting the film in the present, Wegener shot *The Golem* in Germany, rather than in Prague, the setting for his *Student of Prague* (1913).[25] In the scene at the top of the tower, viewers could enjoy the bucolic view of Hildesheim, a town in Lower Saxony that had preserved its medieval façade. The destruction of the golem at the end of the film clears the path for full Jewish acculturation and integration into German society: when Aaron takes the couple in his arms, the viewers can presume that intermarriage ensues. Galeen's overtly Jewish appearance in the film marks him as different, but the screenplay suggests that he does not practice his religion. Instead, he treats the Jewish items in the treasure trove—Shabbat candles, a menorah, an altar covering, and even the golem statue itself—as exotic merchandise with resale value. According to the script, when Aaron receives these items, he "inspects the large altar cloth made out of heavy material, feeling it between his fingers." A smile flits over his face as a title appears: "This is an item for my daughter."[26]

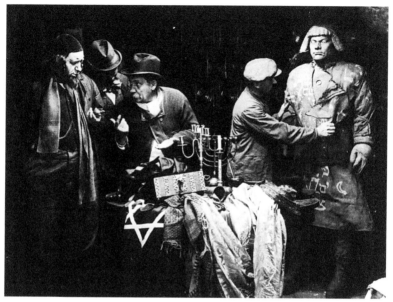

Aaron, the Jewish merchant (left), inspecting the star-shaped capsule.

The film crosscuts to the daughter in her room, secretively reading a letter from the baron, her lover. When Aaron subsequently enters the room with the altar cloth, she looks with amazement at the expensive material, wraps herself with it in front of the mirror, and coquettishly takes a few dance steps. The father shakes his finger at her "but remains cheerful."[27] The assimilatory logic of Wegener's first golem film entails not only this sacrilegious approach to Jewish ritual objects and an affirmation of intermarriage, but also the use of the golem as a found object, accidently animated, rather than a figure in which creative and spiritual efforts are invested.

The expressionist sculptor Rudolph Belling designed the imposing geometric headdress, recalling the stylized hair of ancient Egyptian statues and the shapes of cubist painting and sculpture. The same headdress served Wegener in the 1920s film, although it became longer and fuller, resembling the postwar "bob" (*Bubikopf*) or

American "flapper" hairstyles.[28] The golem's clothing was supposed to recall, by contrast, outfits worn by people "1,000 years ago."[29] The shoulder chains and ropes around the arms conveyed the golem's bondage, and the combination of Hebrew and quasi-cuneiform letters printed on the fabric contributed to the figure's ancient aura. The costume designers removed this latter design element for the 1920 film, set in a fantastic Prague. Pulling from both ancient and modern motifs, the German filmmakers created a golem that showcased the modern fascination with primitive and oriental cultures. In the words of the *Film-Kurier* critic, writing under the byline Andrej, "Paul Wegener enacts this clay-hulk, replicating the most primitive human body . . . a primordial being, between soullessness and animation."[30] Emphasizing Wegener's primitive appearance, this review calls attention to how the golem strips

Publicity photograph of Wegener (right) next to the golem sculpture.
Courtesy of Deutsche Kinemathek, Berlin.

away layers of history and socialization to reflect upon the idea of the human as a "primordial being," especially in the aftermath of extreme trench warfare and the devastating destruction of human life, regardless of national and social background.

In his prefacing speech to the premiere of the 1920 film, Wegener described his first golem film as a "modern societal drama," in contrast to the later film, his "originally intended version," in which he could carry out the grandeur and impact of a stylized period piece.[31] Wegener suggests that while he had developed the conception for the 1920 film already in the 1910s, the medium and its practitioners had not been sufficiently advanced to carry it out. In a 1917 essay, "On the Artistic Possibilities of the Motion Picture" (Von den künstlerischen Möglichkeiten des Wandelbildes), Wegener wrote that "film is, first and foremost, a *visual* matter. The film poet must start with an image, think in images, and choose subjects that can be expressed visually." The subject matter of the golem, an artificial anthropoid brought to life by a rabbi versed in mystical practices, proved itself particularly suitable to such visual expression. As Wegener underscored, the golem was, for him, "the strange stone form that, silently and mystically, unfolded its purely visual existence."[32] In other words, while the golem's animation has been *described* in literary works, because it is a supernatural phenomenon, it can only be *shown* in the realm of film, relying on the camera and its tricks.

If the golem's existence is "purely visual," then this figure could represent cinema itself: like the fleeting moving image, which disappears once the lights are turned on, the golem was, despite its massive body, a ghost of sorts, a figment of cinematic imagination, animated only for the duration of a feature film. In his famous 1913 essay, "Thoughts Toward an Aesthetic of the Cinema," the Hungarian philosopher and critic Georg Lukács focuses on the lack of human presence as the key characteristic of cinema. This lack is not an insufficiency but a stylistic principle, so that cinema can project the "movements and actions of people" but not the people themselves.[33] Film is no less alive for that reason, but its life is elsewhere: it rules over what Lukács designates as a "fantastical" aspect of life that lacks, in its very essence, the presence, causes, and motives characteristic of stage drama. This fantastical life appears to Lukács as soulless, composed of "pure surface," and film becomes thereby a phenomenon of the visual surface; it is "movement in itself," an unbounded, vital flow of images.[34] The golem in its fundamental silence and inhumanity embodies the form of silent cinema, which is, in Lukács's words, an intentionally "soulless" medium, a world of "pure externality" expressed through "actions and gestures."[35]

A modern-day fairy tale, the 1914/1915 film includes a sequence that is particularly emblematic of Lukács's conception of cinema. Titled "Golem's Night Walk" (Golems Nachtgang), the scene has a dreamlike quality, emphasizing "the wonder of the camera." It takes place outdoors, the golem roaming through the city streets, searching for the unruly Jewish daughter. On the golem's way from Aaron's home to the baron's palace to retrieve her, the surrounding nature acts as a distraction. The walk begins in "an old street," proceeds through a "municipal square," and ventures into a park, where the golem enjoys a splash in the pond. At one point it bends over and smells a rose bush, experiencing, as the script succinctly puts it, an "awakening of emotion toward nature."[36]

In German Jewish writer Arnold Zweig's negative review, published in *Die Schaubühne*, *The Golem* "debases" the original legendary materials, since it transposes the narrative to the present day, turning the golem into "a monster, an automaton." However, the "Golem's Night Walk" sequence strikes Zweig as "lyrical," in that "Wegener gives cinema the possibility that no stage can give."[37] In the scene's climax, the golem extends its arms upward to the stars, an "unforgettable image," expressing "amazement," "dull joy," and "trepidation."[38] This self-willed gesture starkly contrasts with the golem's previous heavy and "mechanical" motions, for instance,

The golem of the first film stops to smell a rose.

when Aaron orders it, "Raise your arm!"[39] The nighttime walk shows how the golem might escape from its enslaved, mechanized existence and stages an experience of childlike, wonder-full pleasure, notably following the crass erotic scene with the daughter of the antiques dealer.[40] Through this scene, both the otherwise restrained automaton and cinema itself gain a heightened "poetic" or "fantastic" life, to borrow Lukács's terms.[41] This fantastic life enabled spectators to perceive the newly awakened desires of the mute and monstrous golem, perhaps also moving them to reflect on the conditions of their own humanity.

In deploying the fantastic as both a theme and an inherent quality of the cinematic medium, Wegener emphasized the centrality of trick photography and other special effects. Already in *The Student of Prague*, Wegener used trick photography to play a double role—the student and his ghostly, murderous mirror image. In *The Golem* the cinematography of animation required the substitution of a golem statue or puppet, made of "plaster and paper mâché," for the live actor. The puppet allowed, once more through photographic illusions, the transition from inanimate to animate. For the critic Adolph Behne, these transitions were so "subtly arranged" that it appeared as though "the animated puppet opens its eyes, breathes, moves."[42] Wegener's golem became, in this manner, an animated clay double of the human actor.

In 1920, Wegener continued to explore cinema as a visual surface that allows the filmmaker to project a fantastical sphere. At the same time, together with his co-filmmakers, he wrought significant changes to the narrative, setting, and overall aesthetics of his project. Importantly, Wegener abandoned all German location shots in favor of an entirely fabricated studio setting that integrated the artificial golem into the environment. In the visual context of massive clay ghetto walls and buildings, the emergence of an animated clay giant did not produce the same horrific-comical effects in the later film as it did in the 1914/1915 version. Rather, by 1920, Wegener strove for visual and narrative coherence and overlap across different dimensions of the film: the dramatic plot of magical animation, the golem figure itself, the site of animation or mise-en-scène, and the cinematography of animation. He forged a tactile, three-dimensional aesthetic experience within the boundaries of two-dimensional cinema, thereby striving to uncover the hidden spiritual dimension of the visual surface.

Light and Clay: A Sculptural Aesthetic

As early as 1916, Wegener contended that "rhythm and tempo, light and darkness have a role to play in film, as they do in music."[43] In his vision of cinema as a form of "kinetic lyricism," the "factual or realistic image" (*Tatsachenbild*) would ultimately be renounced.[44] With the help of the German Jewish cinematographer Karl Freund, who went on to film Fritz Lang's *Metropolis* in 1927, the 1920 film

The first shot of *The Golem, How He Came into the World.*

ambitiously set out to locate the golem plot in the context of a lyrical exploration of light and shadow. Moreover, each frame of the film was tinted in post-production. The filmmakers used a variety of shades ranging from blues and greens to soft pink, sepia, and even orange-red, in order to distinguish between night and day, court and ghetto, enhancing the drama and atmosphere of the film.

In the opening shot of Wegener's 1920 film, tinted blue for a nighttime effect, viewers can make out the silhouettes of what appear to be jagged cliffs, but subsequently emerge as the tops of the ghetto structures. One of these architectural forms is a tower, and, above it, the image pulls our gaze toward a group of stars that are particularly large and luminous, forming a constellation. In the next low-angle shot, Rabbi Loew (enacted by Albert Steinrück) appears on this tower above his home, peering into a telescope that cuts across the frame. Viewers then contemplate an iris shot, representing Rabbi

Rabbi Loew peers through his telescope at the night sky.

Iris shot of the constellations through the telescope.

Loew's own gaze through the telescope. Through the tower and the human figure with its telescope, Freund framed the night sky, which bears an ominous message for the Jewish community.

The first shots establish the correlation between the clay and wood constructions of the ghetto and the ethereal elements, or between human and heavenly forces, a link that carries over to the figure of the clay golem. In the words of the 1920 *Film-Kurier* critic Andrej: "Like the earth and sea, the golem is mysteriously connected to the constellation of the stars, which make him at times wild and at times meek: ebb and flow."[45] The rabbi initially decides to create the golem after reading the stars and determining that a disaster is impending; he also summons up the "terrible Astaroth," a demonic spirit, but does not force it to reveal the "magic word" that animates the golem until "Venus enters the constellation." Similarly, after the golem has fulfilled its mission, the rabbi discovers that "when Uranus enters the house of the planets," the golem will become destructive, ruled by the vengeful Astaroth again.[46] The narrative of *The Golem, How He Came into the World* follows, in this manner, an astrological logic, and the film exhibits an "ebb and flow," a poetic rhythm alternating between narrative-driven and more visually dictated constellations of shots.

On a cinematic level, Freund projected this astrological logic through lighting effects. The contrast between shadows and bright stars dominate the first shots. After the rabbi understands the import of the stars, the next shot brings us into his home, where a young assistant (*Famulus*, in German, or famulus, in archaic English) stares at glass flasks, suggestive of alchemical experiments. This green-tinted shot that introduces us to the character of the famulus—enacted by Ernst Deutsch, who later played the lead role in E. A. Dupont's *The Ancient Law* (*Das alte Gesetz*, 1923)—lasts fifteen seconds, an excessive amount of time in terms of narrative progression. A bright ray of light enters the frame from the right, illuminating the flasks and part of the famulus's face, but the rest of

Stark light and dark effects.

the room is shrouded in darkness. In his interpretation of the film's chiaroscuro lighting, Frances Guerin writes that "the mise-en-scène is reduced to a pattern in light and darkness."[47]

Another scene from early on in the film further cements the correlation between lighting effects and the clay of both the golem and the ghetto. As Rabbi Loew enters an underground, sealed room, where he consults plans and molds the figure of the golem, viewers see the shadow cast by the rabbi on the wall of this underground space beside three blueprints for the golem—schematic drawings of the anthropoid's contours surrounded by notations and letters. The yet-to-be-formed clay on the left side of the frame provides here a tactile, even sensuous complement to the flatness of the drawings and the shadow on the wall. Because of the dramatic lighting effects, as well as the position of the camera, Rabbi Loew merges with his

Rabbi Loew's shadow cast on the wall next to the unformed golem.

creation: his shadow on the wall fits within the outlines of the golem, and, since his own body is absent from the frame, the creator appears as the ghostly counterpart of the soulless clay object. Through these lighting and framing effects, the film suggests that animation is a cinematic event, a product of the play of light and shadows, transforming a kind of script (consisting of images and text) into live action and motion.

Through crosscutting, the filmmakers extended the rabbi's action of kneading the clay. A medium shot shows him at work; the film then crosscuts to the delivery of the expulsion edict from the court to one of the Jewish elders, and once again back to the rabbi. A close-up on his hands, with the rest of the room cast in shadow, shows the rabbi vigorously plying the unformed matter. The film then cuts to the imperial messenger, as the ghetto Jews show him the way to the rabbi's home. We see the rabbi complete his work on the golem and reseal the room. The prolonged process of kneading, enhanced through crosscutting, reminds viewers that although the finished golem appears to have a smooth exterior, the rabbi has formed this figure out of coarse and malleable clay through extensive labor.

The shots of kneading focus on the golem's face alone, whereas the body appears already formed. In this manner, Wegener underscores the significance of the face for his filmmaking. Hungarian film theorist and writer Béla Balázs considered the facial close-up the epitome of cinematic expressivity, affording, in Noa Steimatzky's words, a "liberat[ion] from linear and spatial calculation, from succession and progression."[48] Rather than operating in a well-defined space, the isolation and enlargement of a face on the screen

Rabbi Loew molding the golem's face.

allows viewers to lose their awareness of space, opening up a "new dimension": "physiognomy."[49] Subjective emotions and thoughts made visible through facial expressions constitute, for Balázs, a "spiritual dimension."[50] The cinematic face allows us to see and recognize the human spirit on the surface of things. In the clay-kneading sequence, we see a close-up of a face that has not yet been formed. It isolates the rabbi's hands and golem's clay against the backdrop of the two-dimensional sketch. The shot both slows down the progression of the narrative taking place outside the rabbi's home (the delivery of the edict) and creates an intense anticipation for the emergence of a fully formed face. The kneading of the clay face reveals the multilayered nature of film's physiognomy, suggesting that cinema does not merely record faces but creatively participates in molding its own "spiritual dimension." These shots inform the multiple subsequent close-ups on the golem's expressions, becoming the vehicle and medium through which the filmmakers express the anthropoid's transformation.

The transition from a two-dimensional scheme to a three-dimensional sculpture, and from raw material to a formed shape, epitomizes the overall aesthetic thrust of the 1920 film. In the opening sequence of the second act, prior to the golem's animation, three shallow shots dissolve into one another. First, the starry night sky from the very beginning of the film reappears, though no longer framed by the ghetto towers from below, and then dissolves into an image of a Star of David, which finally dissolves into a close-up of the golem, eyes closed, unmoving. The facial close-up functions here as the expressive counterpart to the more abstract Star of David. At the same time, the Star of David itself displays multiple dimensions in this scene: it shifts from a tactile object made of clay to a flatter, brighter image and then reverts to thick clay as it dissolves over Wegener's face.

The enhancement of the pulsating star is indicative of a dimension that exists within and beyond the flat surface of things. The

The Star of David transforms from a three-dimensional to a two-dimensional image.

The clay Star of David superimposed on the golem's expectant face.

hexagram—itself a symbol that historically was used by Jews and non-Jews for both ornamental and magical ends—mediates between the earthbound golem in the Jewish ghetto and the sphere of the heavens with its symbolic stars and messages.[51] Through dissolve, close-up, and superimposition, Wegener suggests that cinema itself can affect the magical transition from the two-dimensional to the three-dimensional, from the flat surface to the tactile object.

The dissolve of three distinct shots creates a kind of triptych in motion, a Christian aesthetic format visually suited to this scene that foretells the impending "birth" of the golem-savior through the appearance of a star. At the end of the film, when superimposed on a shot of the closed ghetto gate, the hexagram further represents the Jewish community in its regained security and independence. The Star of David is a kind of seal on the gate, marking Prague Jewry's isolation from the surrounding Christian world. While the filmmakers used this extradiegetic symbol superimposed on the film to highlight the golem's multiple communal functions as savior and shield, audiences of the period would also have been aware of the modern uses of the Star of David. Starting with the 1897 Zionist Congress, the star had come to symbolize the Zionist movement and its hopes for the political and cultural redemption of the Jews of Europe. German Jewish artists, such as the poet Else Lasker-Schüler, had adopted the Star of David in order "to disclose Jewishness and to avoid passive acceptance of the Jewishness projected onto them by others," in Kerry Wallach's words.[52] As a symbol of Jewish visibility and potential national self-assertion and territorialization, the Star of David invited its viewers to consider how the hermetic world of the cinematic ghetto might stand in dialogue with present-day transformations within assimilated German Jewish society. The fantastic ghetto of the film, in which the Jews foster a tight-knit community, is also, in this vein, a utopian homeland, a yet-unrealized dream, rather than an imagined ghetto of the past.

Poelzig's "Golem City"

As an overdetermined symbol, the Star of David corresponds to the filmmakers' overall use of architecture and design to project both modern and antiquated, utopian and fantastic spaces. Unlike the earlier golem films, *The Golem, How He Came into the World* distances the world of the golem from everyday life, creating a fully enclosed, entirely imagined sphere in which foreground and background, the animate and the inanimate, could become expressive. Whereas the 1914/1915 and 1917 films combined indoor studio settings with outdoor shots on location, the 1920 film omitted all outdoor locations. In its attempt to create an enclosed and artificial cinematic space, this film may be compared with Robert Wiene's groundbreaking *The Cabinet of Dr. Caligari*, which premiered in February 1920. However, while Wiene's film was indebted to exaggerated expressionist acting styles on the German stage as well as to flat, hand-painted expressionist set design, recent scholarship distinguishes Wegener's film from the all-encompassing aesthetic of expressionism.[53] In Dietrich Scheunemann's view, for instance, the interior and exterior sets for *The Golem, How He Came into the World* are stylistically anti-naturalist, owing more to art nouveau than to expressionist painting.[54]

The flat and painted sets of *The Cabinet of Dr. Caligari* reveal a strong affinity to Cubism: they create, in Anton Kaes's words, a "camouflage effect in which foreground and background mesh," reducing the depth of the image and causing the characters to blend into the scenery.[55] For Eugen Tannenbaum, who attended the film's premiere in Berlin, Wegener's landmark film forged a new relationship to modern art, but unlike *The Cabinet of Dr. Caligari*, which ties in with expressionist painting, *The Golem, How He Came into the World* stands in relationship to the "fantastic architecture of symbol-laden sculpture."[56] In scenes like the molding of the golem or the superimposition of the Star of David upon the golem's face, Wegener utilizes two-dimensional, flat or painterly settings, as in

The two-dimensional painted facades of *The Cabinet of Dr. Caligari*.

Wiene's *Caligari*, but his ultimate goal is to show how characters and objects attain a three-dimensional form, expressive of the magic of animation. The animation of the inanimate goes hand in hand, in *The Golem, How He Came into the World*, with the projection of three-dimensional spaces on the two-dimensional screen. In other words, a sculptural aesthetic, rather than a pictorial one, dominates Wegener's film, in an effort to convey the presence of a deeper, hidden meaning or message underlying the visual surface.

The sets of *The Golem* present a strong contrast to *Caligari*'s painted canvas sets. While the set designs of both films are antimimetic, avoiding any realistic resemblances, Hans Poelzig designed for Wegener's film a "golem city," a habitable space that was entirely constructed and fantastic. "Nobody ever lived in a ghetto like the one pictured in 'The Golem,'" a New York Tribune critic recognized at the outset of a 1921 review that situated this cinematic ghetto at the center of the film's "action."[57] For critic Herbert Ihering, these same attributes heralded a new epoch for cinema: "Wegener and Poelzig proved that only the tightly structured, rhythmically concentrated image, one that eliminates all the accidental qualities of nature, opens the future for film."[58] The Ufa film company (Universum Film AG)—founded in 1917 with German government support, following the direct encouragement of General Erich Ludendorff—had the resources necessary to construct an entire model ghetto at its Tempelhof studios.[59] Poelzig, an architect renowned for the stalactite-like interior of the Great Theater in Berlin, designed all fifty-four buildings of the "golem city." His partner, sculptor Marlene Moeschke, modeled these constructs, and Kurt Richter built them.[60]

The narrowness of the ghetto streets and the asymmetry of the homes contributed to the magical atmosphere in which an artificial

Hans Poelzig's sets: publicity photograph of a square.
Courtesy of Deutsches Filminstitut Frankfurt / Sammlung Kai Möller.

creation might be brought to life and also revealed how the cities of the future could be threatening, dwarfing their human inhabitants. In order to create such effects, Poelzig drew heavily on historical architectural elements: the vertically striving arches of his inner and outer constructs created gothic effects. Claudia Dillmann considers these arches and bows the "keynote of the mystical tone, in which the golem-city, the imagined Prague ghetto of the 16th century . . . would sing and lament."[61] Poelzig also used the gothic verticality to suggest that the homes of the ghetto were leaning towards each other, their ogival roofs creating further arches in the spaces between them, accentuated by bridges.[62] Poelzig designed the palace of Rudolph II as a gothic counterpart to the ghetto that exhibits an ornamental, classic design, its hall filled with gothic tracery, adorned with flower motifs. While the court space, inhabited by the emperor and his entourage, is symmetrical and ornamentalized, a space in

Gothic motifs in the interior design of the Prague court.

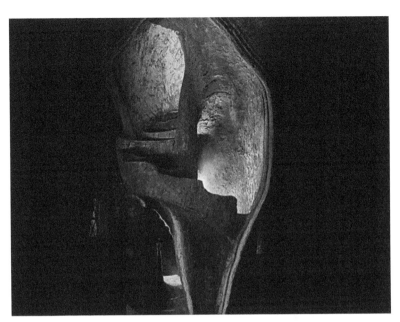

Rabbi Loew descending the biomorphic stairs inside his home.

which frivolous celebrations take place, the Jewish ghetto is a site of creativity and consequence, a space in which a golem can be animated through spiritual and magical ritual. The gothic spirit shaping the ghetto is "dynamic" and "striving" rather than static and decadent.[63]

Wegener's film stylizes nature in more than one respect: the artificial studio setting of the film has a lifelike quality with its organic shapes and twisted forms, enhancing the animation of the clay golem as it awakens to life and its emotional forces. Made of clay, brick, and straw, the ghetto buildings corresponded to the clay matter of the golem itself—a shared materiality of structures and monster. Additionally, the curves and stalactite forms in the interiors echoed the shapes of the human body and its cavities, suggesting not only a continuum between golem and ghetto, but also between the human inhabitants and their living environments.[64] In contrast to the mimetic indoor spaces of the earlier films—especially the antique shop (1914/1915) and the dancer's boudoir (1917)—and the outdoor settings of Hildesheim, the 1920 mise-en-scène did not strive to imitate our own world but rather "realized the unreal" by projecting an enclosed fantasy world that nonetheless borrowed and stylized natural and gothic elements.[65]

Another central architectural element in the film is the wall that surrounds the ghetto and the gargantuan gate that leads to and from this space. The first time this wall appears in view, through a long shot, it exceeds the boundaries of the frame so that we cannot visually measure its height and length. The thick wall dwarfs the imperial messenger on horseback. Reduced in stature, the messenger, a young nobleman named Florian, rings a bell, and the old watchman runs down from a tower atop the wall to open a wicket gate embedded in the larger one. Only when catching sight of the imperial seal does

The nobleman, Florian, arrives at the ghetto bearing the edict.

The gatekeeper pulls the giant crossbar.

the gatekeeper proceed to pull on a rope that lowers the enormous crossbar securing the twenty-foot-tall wooden gate. Significantly, the hinge upon which this long piece of wood rotates resembles the star-shaped capsule into which Rabbi Loew, in a subsequent scene, places the animating word that brings the golem to life. Both stars need to revolve in order for the door or the golem to move, to come to life. The golem's animation becomes linked, through this graphically matching prop, to infringement on the ghetto's isolation, as represented by its barred door.

In the last minutes of the film, when the golem's anger has been spent and it looks out of the ghetto door's peephole, it sees Christian children dancing in circles, flowers adorning their hair, and proceeds to break out of the ghetto and join them. Through sheer force, the golem pushes the door open, breaking the crossbar

The golem breaks the ghetto gate and its crossbar.

in half. At this point in the film, after the emperor has annulled the edict of expulsion and allowed the Jews of Prague to continue to reside in the ghetto, the golem's action is highly symbolic. Its creation and animation took place in tandem with the imperial messenger's arrival in the ghetto. By way of departure from the ghetto, the golem tears down the massive door separating the Jewish population from their Christian neighbors. In contrast to the 1914/1915 film, in the 1920 version, Galeen and Wegener do not portray Jewish assimilation as a desirable outcome. On the contrary, the golem throws Florian, who has become the daughter's lover, off the top of the tower. The film restores thereby a sense of ethnoreligious order. The broken crossbar reminds us, at the same time, that complete isolation and segregation have led this community to the brink of expulsion and disaster.

Poelzig's film architecture left a deep impression on contemporary viewers. German Jewish art historian Paul Westheim noted, in 1920, the gothic dimension of Poelzig's designs: a "blaze-up of flaming, quivering, lambent striving forces." Rather than the magic of ruins, Westheim contended, the architecture had "its own life, a life that a master-builder's spirit has projected into it . . . under the hands of the modeler, the inert lumps [*Massen*] have become expressive, they have been given momentum, a gesture, a face."[66] The *New York Times* review of the film similarly instructed its spectators to view the "massive" and "unearthly" settings as "as active a part of the story as any of the characters." These "expressive settings . . . vivify the action of the story," bringing it to life in much the same way that Rabbi Loew models and brings the golem to life.[67]

Underpinning both past and present interpretations of the spatial-material aspect of *The Golem, How He Came into the World* is the notion that Poelzig's set design exhibited the Jewishness of the Prague ghetto's inhabitants. As both Poelzig and contemporaneous critics maintained, the architecture "actively expresses" itself through the Jewish-inflected speech of the homes, their "mauscheln" (a derogatory term for the Jewish pronunciation of German).[68] In Gustav Meyrink's bestselling novel of 1915 *Der Golem*, which provided inspiration to both Wegener and Poelzig, the ghetto and its homes convey sinister degeneration and engage in "ghostly" and "mysterious counsel together."[69] However, while Poelzig's fantastic ghetto forges a dialogue between gothic and organic architectural elements, his set designs did not project a sense of uncanny depravity. For writer Herman Scheffauer, the setting displayed "a kind of Jewish Gothic" that blended the "flame-like letters of the Jewish alphabet with the leaf-like flames of Gothic tracery."[70] This notion of a "Jewish gothic" might have been inspired by the posters for the film, designed by Poelzig as well, which showed fingers of fire rising from the ghetto buildings and merging into the title of the film in German, drawn in elongated, crooked letters. The German architecture critic Heinrich

Hans Poelzig's poster for *The Golem, How He Came into the World.*

de Fries observed that the "Jewish gothic" of the set design created a tight, inseparable association between plot and space.[71]

More recently, Noah Isenberg has argued that the ethnic coding of the ghetto space as Jewish evoked for German viewers images of the influx of Eastern European Jews to Germany during and after World War I. He describes the crowds of Jews filling the ghetto spaces as "amorphous" and "swarming," arguing that the Jewish spaces exhibit "distorted shapes, dark cavities, and hunchbacked structures."[72] Mass scenes from the last third of the film, when the golem sets fire to the ghetto and the Jews rush out to the streets to avoid being trapped in their homes, reveal such swarming, albeit narratively justified.

Other scenes, by contrast, are not shot from such an exaggeratedly high angle that traps the Jewish population between leaning structures, but rather from a straighter or slightly tilted angle, with

Jewish masses in the streets of the burning ghetto.

the homes serving as background. These kinds of shots integrate the Jewish population into the built environment in a non-demeaning manner. In a still from the last minutes of the film, the shadows cast by the ghetto buildings on the ghetto wall graphically match the pointed black hats forced upon medieval male Jews, accentuating the commonality of human attire and home. Rather than perceive this visual effect as intensifying the antisemitic connotations of the ghetto space, we might also view it as an appropriation of the pointed hat. This prop becomes, through the repetition of the shadows, far more dynamic and expressive, suggestive of Jewishness as an internally animating force rather than as an identity enforced from the outside.

From the opening shots of the film, the clay golem and the ghetto are bound up with the elements of sky and stars that both propel the plot forward and enhance the film's symbolic dimension. Poelzig

Rabbi Loew (front right) surrounded by his community in the ghetto.

and Wegener thus forged novel configurations of atavistic *and* utopic elements. The fantasy suggested by the film's "golem city" reminded viewers of their own cityscapes and the threats found within them, but also, simultaneously, transported them to other, dreamlike worlds and unimaginable spaces. As Andrej wrote, "No history, but a dream of a faraway past . . ."[73] In Wegener's own words, Poelzig's "alleys and squares should not remind one of anything in reality; they should create the atmosphere in which the golem breathes."[74]

Cinematic Jewishness

The intertwinement of history and fiction, dream and reality in Wegener's production extends beyond the film's architecture to include the overall depiction of Jewish society in relationship to the majority Christian society. In *The Golem* of 1914/1915, Wegener and Galeen characterize the Jewish antique dealer and his daughter as social strivers who seek to attain a higher status through assimilation and romantic alliance. Similarly, in Dupont's 1923 film *The Ancient Law*, what seem to be insurmountable differences between Jews and Christians in Central Europe—differences, in Valerie Weinstein's words, of "space, class, and culture"—are overcome. However, *The Ancient Law* also ambivalently portrays assimilation as both an act of dislocation (from Galicia to Vienna) and as familial reunification in this new context.[75] Dupont's film, for Cynthia Walk, "promot[es] acculturation within limits that preserve Jewish distinctiveness and loyalty to ethnic heritage," disavowing intermarriage but allowing the violation of Jewish law, such as that of Yom Kippur observation.[76] Screened only a few years prior to *The Ancient Law*, *The Golem, How He Came into the World* swerves away from the clear-cut assimilation narrative of the first golem film and does not promote any version of Jewish acculturation. The Jews living in the ghetto of Wegener's 1920 film form a self-sufficient society that appears uninterested in relations with its Christian neighbors.

One exception is the character of Miriam, the rabbi's daughter (Lyda Salmonova). In contrast to the daughter in the 1914/1915 film, who escapes her home to meet the baron, Miriam never leaves the ghetto, and she conducts her love affair with the nobleman Florian (Lothar Müthel) inside the home. The image of Miriam as seductress, or "femme fatale," contrasts with that of the other women in the ghetto, who dress modestly with covered hair.[77] While the Christian women at the court are likewise flirtatious, their costumes are European, whereas Miriam wears long silky garbs that trail below her feet, and her hair is braided and adorned. As Wallach has shown, "racialized coding . . . was common in mainstream Weimar contexts," leading, at times, to false perceptions of dark-haired women as Jewish.[78] Miriam's ethnoracial coding relies on her long, dark hair, which, later on, turns into a rope of sorts that the golem uses to drag her through the streets.

Florian, the Christian nobleman, and Miriam, the rabbi's daughter.

Miriam, the rabbi's daughter, coquettishly peering out the window.

The orientalist stylization of Miriam's costume, through pearl earrings, a turban-like headdress, and billowy clothing, goes hand in hand with the conception of the golem as an orientalist object in all three films. In the 1914/1915 *Der Golem*, the clay monster is but one of many oriental items in the Jewish dealer's shop; one reviewer characterized this figure as a combination of a demonic "oriental idol" and a heroic "Roland statue," a European military figure.[79] Critics deemed Wegener suitable to enact the golem, since he supposedly represented the "Mongolian type," with his "wide, angular face" and slanted "Mongolian eyes."[80] The co-director of the third golem film, Carl Boese, commented that Wegener's "physiognomy, with its Alpine or at least Slavic note" served the task of embodying the golem in all its power.[81] In addition to the costume design and dark-toned makeup, Wegener's own colleagues coded him as inherently "other," based upon his physical features. The "backwardness and brutality" of the golem evoked, according to Daniel Wildmann, the "other side of orientalist fantasies," thereby complementing the feminine oriental appeal of Miriam.[82] The differing orientalist fashioning of these two characters also manifests in their behavior: whereas Miriam exhibits an excessively emotional demeanor, the golem initially appears unwavering, stone-like. Orientalized and gendered differently, both figures nevertheless mark cinematic Jewishness as excessive, transgressive, and threatening. The film uses the outward appearance and demeanor of the Jews and their creations to justify Christian desire for and fear of the Jewish other.

These orientalist tendencies of the film reinforce the characterization of the ghetto as a mystical space and its rabbi as an occult master. In addition to the silent film intertitles, *The Golem* includes several shots of manuscripts or scrolls, which underscore the importance of the written word.[83] Early on in the film, a scroll shot reveals a list of Jewish transgressions, including the crucifixion, disregard for Christian holidays, endangering of lives and property, and the practice of "black arts" or "magic" (*schwarze Künste*). Ironically, in order to defend his community against these accusations, Rabbi Loew must delve into "necromancy" (conjuring demons) and artificial creation. Significantly, in Wegener's adaptation, we do not see Loew consulting any Jewish mystical treatises, and golem-making becomes, in another intertitle, associated with "Thessaly" or ancient Greece, rather than with Jewish antiquity. In the scene in which Loew forces the demon, Astaroth, to divulge the magical word, *Aemaet* (German transliteration of the Hebrew *emet*, truth), that animates the golem, he fittingly wears a magician's hat rather than the pointed *Judenhut* (Jewish hat). As a low-angle shot establishes, Rabbi Loew stands tall, waving his wand and drawing a circle of fire around himself and the famulus. When flames appear out of nowhere and dance on the walls, the famulus partially collapses while the rabbi struggles to keep his eyes open, holding a large pentagram to protect himself, and calling upon Astaroth to "name the word."

The ways in which the rabbi uses the pentagram in the scene with the demon recall the doctrine of Eliphas Levi, a nineteenth-century

Rabbi Loew protects himself with a three-dimensional pentagram.

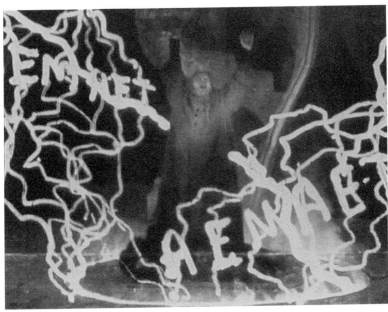

The word *Aemaet* (truth) etched into the lightning bolts.

French occultist. Levi maintained that the pentagram, a "blazing star," was "the sign of intellectual omnipotence and autocracy." In the film, Rabbi Loew holds one point up, hinting at his role as creator of the golem-savior. Since the pentagram "terrifies phantoms" but welcomes good spirits, the rabbi uses it to ward off the danger of the demon whom he has conjured up.[84] After the word appears as a trail of smoke emanating from the demon's mask, the rabbi lays the unconscious assistant on the ground and a storm of thunderbolts swirls around him, culminating in a strong explosion that knocks the rabbi down as well. This scene entailed multiple types of superimposition, as well as skilled use of fire and smoke. It was technically challenging, as Carl Boese, who was not only co-director but also responsible for special effects, later attested.[85] Within the thunderbolts, the filmmakers embedded the word *Aemaet*, which Astaroth had previously revealed. First a word written in smoke, it now appears etched in light, thereby becoming a fully cinematic term, one that animates by capturing light on film.

As we have seen in the case of the multivalent ghetto set, Rabbi Loew's Jewishness expresses itself, in this scene and others, not merely through his magic, but also through his bravery and willingness to risk his life to protect his community. By contrast, the famulus embodies the stereotype of the effeminate, weak, and nervous Jewish man, unable to withstand the terror of encountering the demon. The famulus also functions as the third wheel in the ensuing romantic drama—when he later realizes that Miriam is hiding Florian in her bedroom, he animates the golem in order to do the work of revenge for him. In contrast to Rabbi Loew, who uses the golem only to protect his community from expulsion, the famulus employs the golem for his personal advantage, ultimately forcing Miriam into a socially sanctioned relationship. The varied landscape of male and female affect, appearance, and behavior within the Jewish community shows how the film exploited racial codes and, simultaneously, depicted the ghetto Jews as resilient and creative, traits epitomized by their leader. Ultimately, this community manages to defend itself from attacks originating both from without and from within, using a combination of belief, magic, and bravery.

The Clay of War

The lightning storm that takes place inside the rabbi's home evokes, albeit implicitly, the World War I battlefield, in which soldiers hid in clay dugouts while artillery raged all around them. They were not, however, protected by magical circles of flames or pentagrams, but rather endured the proximity of the enemy and its deadly weapons without a strong line of defense, relying oftentimes on sheer luck for survival. Wegener was one of the fortunate ones, but he did not remain unscathed by his experiences on the front lines. In 1933, the actor published an account of his service entitled *Flanders Diary*

Paul Wegener in the trenches (front left). Courtesy of
the Deutsches Filminstitut Frankfurt / Sammlung Kai Möller.

1914 (Flandrisches Tagebuch 1914); he also recorded his travails as
they were taking place, in letters he wrote to his friend Ernst Pietsch
and notes made in his soldier's identification and pay book.

In October 1914, after volunteering for the *Landsturm*, Wegener
marched through the Belgian city of Diksmuide, in West Flanders,
arriving at the front lines in mid-October.[86] On December 2, 1914, he
wrote to Pietsch that although "one is dulled [to death and injury], it
is nonetheless no small thing to spend days and nights in such close
proximity to the enemy, in clay trenches without food, with death
always nearby."[87] In the region of the Yser River, where Wegener's
company was located, "the distance between Belgians and Germans
was at times just a few yards of wet mud."[88] Wegener repeatedly
noted his mood in those days as "deeply depressed" (deprimierte

GERMAN FILM CLASSICS

Stimmung or tiefe Depression) and his state as one of despondency (Mutlosigkeit bei mir).[89] After a senseless attack that took place in mid-October 1914, he also wrote how a sentiment of "mistrust" had arisen among the soldiers toward their leadership. He called the wounded and deceased soldiers "the poor victims of these days" who "paid with their lives and are irreplaceable."[90]

On December 4, Wegener's company came under heavy bombardment, causing the deaths of almost his entire squad. He depicted the battle as "a constant howling and cracking," with the enemy shooting grenades, volleys, and shrapnel. "The ground shook so hard it literally felt like an earthquake. . . . It lasted for one and a half hours without cessation. We all sat utterly silent [*stumm*] and waited for the end. Every one of us felt the proximity of death; earth, grenade splinter, and smoke filled our dugout." When the bombardment slowed down, Wegener tried to haul those still alive out of their "holes."[91] Later when he returned to the dugout, he could no longer find his comrades, only a giant grenade hole. As he traversed the trench, Wegener climbed over wounded and dead soldiers, noting that the ceiling and walls were covered with blood and brains. Still, he wrote, "one is strangely indifferent."[92] The numbing of emotional response served Wegener as a defense mechanism, recalling the apathy of the golem character that he would return to embody in two further films. A traditionally mute entity, the golem also symbolically represented the muteness of those soldiers awaiting the end of their lives in the trenches.

Writing to Pietsch on December 9, shortly after these events, Wegener called the day of the Yser battle "the most atrocious day of my life." He described the "boredom of the modern defense war" and its "senseless murder" as "positively absurd."[93] In this and subsequent letters, Wegener noted his lack of any joy or hope—"The worst thing is the hopelessness!" (Das schlimmste ist die Hoffnunglosigkeit!)— and his sense of guilt at being alive.[94] Despite being awarded the Iron Cross First Class, Wegener declared that he hadn't performed any heroic deeds, that he simply acted "out of fear" or because he was "ordered to do so."[95] Following these harrowing battles, Wegener endured, in January of 1915, what he called "an acute nervous heart weakness" and received a two-week-long convalescence in Germany. He then returned to the front lines but suffered a relapse. In another letter to Pietsch, the actor explained that he had no physical heart problems like palpitations, only a "nervous atony of the heart muscle as a result of the great exertion and agitation of the first few months [of service]." Wegener's symptoms included spells of dizziness, trouble walking, and a constant "dull, languid feeling."[96] More than any physical injury, he suffered from psychiatric trauma, which left him both physically exhausted and mentally weak.

Shortly after Wegener underwent these harrowing experiences on the battlefield, his first golem film premiered to much acclaim in Berlin. On January 15, 1915, the day after the premiere, Wegener's essay "Acting and Film" (Schauspielerei und Film) was printed in the daily newspaper *Berliner Tageblatt*, with the following preface: "Paul Wegener, Lieutenant and Knight of the Iron Cross first class is at the moment importantly occupied in Flanders, although yesterday he gave a guest performance in effigy as author and actor in a Berlin film theater."[97] At this point in his service, Wegener had already reported his heart condition, but for German audiences, his image was that of a decorated soldier, a hero.[98] The Swiss journalist Eduard Korrodi also remarked in 1915 that only "under strange circumstances" could audiences see Wegener at the movie theater while he was "sacrificing his body and soul and his human voice to his fatherland . . . as lieutenant."[99] For the first time since the invention of cinema, audiences consumed the moving images of actors whose very existence was compromised at the war front or who might even be dead. While the cinematic medium resurrected Wegener, who by dint of his service on the front lines literally wavered between life and death, this reappearance, for Korrodi, could only be partial and unreal. Significantly, on the screen, Wegener embodied a clay monster, removed from a trench-like hole in the ground, and animated only for a brief period of time in order to serve its master.

Metonymically, the golem's clay body recalled the trenches themselves, dug out of the earth. In a note jotted down in his soldier's pay book, Wegener described himself, in the trenches, as "boiling in clay the entire day" (den ganzen Tag in Lehm kochen).[100] As a living-dead entity, whose existence is controlled by others, the golem represented the modern soldier on the World War I battlefield, condemned to an unknown, oftentimes brutal fate. While the first golem film, produced prior to Wegener's service, did not stand in direct dialogue with his war experiences, his final golem project of 1920 exhibits traces of the war and its aftermath. As film scholar Anton Kaes has claimed, the major German films of the 1920s can be considered "shell shock cinema": although they do not show military combat, they "restage the shock of war and defeat" through their narratives and images. Kaes emphasizes the role of the crime and horror genres in Weimar cinema, which showcased communities and individuals in severe distress, exuding "a sense of paranoia and panic." Visually, these films "mimic shock and violence" through extreme lighting effects and abrupt editing techniques.[101] Rather than approaching the war events directly—an attempt bound to disappoint because of its lack of authenticity—*The Golem, How He Came into the World* "restages the shock of war" by creating an atmosphere of horror and dread, amplified through the film's use of space, lighting, and special effects.[102]

Susanne Holl and Friedrich Kittler have maintained that as a result of his World War I service, Wegener transformed the 1920 golem from a servant-guardian into a "weapon" or even a "new automatic weapon system." This golem embodied the kind of worker-soldier that World War I demanded: it did not experience nervous breakdowns and could handle catastrophic explosions with equanimity.[103] In addition, by humanizing the golem in ways that far exceeded the Night Walk scene of the 1914/1915 film,

Wegener extended to viewers a vision of postwar recovery. Holl and Kittler consider the 1920 golem a fantasy projection, attempting to compensate for Wegener's inability to fulfill the role of the undaunted soldier. When approaching the 1920 film as "shell shock cinema," however, we need to account not only for the golem's stoicism and the atmosphere of war and terror, but also for this figure's development over the course of the film. Rather than a mere "weapon system" that defends Jews from the threat of expulsion, the 1920 golem is an animated, evolving being that ultimately attains a semblance of humanity. When brought to court, the golem appears oblivious to the chaos around it and prevents the ceiling from collapsing. Yet as the golem's consciousness of and appreciation for life grows, so does its comprehension of death and its desire to control the capsule that animates it. When the rabbi decides to end the golem's existence after the emperor annuls the expulsion decree against the Jews, the golem attempts to prevent him from doing so by covering the star-shaped capsule with its hand. This same self-protective gesture occurs later when the rabbi's assistant regrets his decision to animate the golem and tries to remove the capsule. The automaton's growing desire to remain "alive" recalls Wegener's own close brushes with death.

As we have seen, in the 1920 film, Wegener sought to intensify the expressiveness and vivaciousness of the entire film design, and not just of the golem character. Within this expressive mise-en-scène, the drama of impending Jewish exile and the rabbi's battle to protect his community enlist the audience's sympathies. Unlike the soldiers waiting mutely, helplessly in the trenches, the Jews of Prague place their fate in the hands of their own spiritual leader, Rabbi Loew. The Christian emperor (a stand-in for the "German Kaiser," according to Holl and Kittler) reacts callously to the suffering of the Jews and even his own people.[104] His style of leadership recalls the lack of empathy exhibited by commanders toward the death of individual soldiers, as noted in Wegener's published diary.[105] Rather than simply reproduce the war and its

The Golem grows angry as the rabbi tries to remove his animating capsule.

destructive weapons, the postwar golem film reflected upon them critically, forging an ethical roadmap for a traumatized society.

Combat at Court

At the climax of the film, Rabbi Loew is invited to court during the Rose Festival in order to display his "magical arts," revealing how the Christian court hypocritically sanctions and enjoys Jewish magic. In the invitation, the word "black" has been omitted, but the term "*Künste*" (arts) still appears, hinting at Loew's occult practices. At court, the rabbi acts as a modern film director, projecting on one of the walls a scene of ancient Israelites wandering in the desert. The textual source for this scene is Leopold Weisel's mid-nineteenth-century Prague story, collected in the Bohemian Jewish collection of tales, *Sippurim*. In this narrative, the emperor bids Rabbi Loew to raise his ancestors from the dead, and the rabbi agrees to conjure them up on the condition that the emperor does not laugh, no matter what he sees. To the "greatness and strength of the men of antiquity," who appear in the foreground, Wegener added the masses of Israelites, exiled and wandering in the desert.[106] As in Weisel's story, the rabbi warns the court not to speak or laugh (in other words, to be somewhat golem-like) when viewing the spectacle, "or else a dreadful disaster [*Unheil*] might take place."

When a distraught, long-bearded figure comes stumbling to the forefront, the court jester makes a remark that causes a ripple of laughter to pass through the audience. As if responding to this display, the man in the image, identified as Ahasverus, the Wandering Jew, walks rapidly toward them, looming larger and larger, appearing

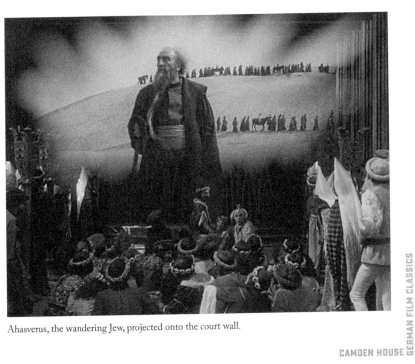

Ahasverus, the wandering Jew, projected onto the court wall.

to walk into the hall. The "film-within-a-film" ends in an explosion of light, and the ceiling of the smoke-filled hall plummets to the ground.[107] Both the wandering Jew and the golem are living-dead, condemned to exist with little control over their own lives and fates. When the spectators refuse to recognize the misfortunes of these living-dead exiles, as preserved by the haunting visual medium of film, their own lives are also endangered. Since the golem blocks the only exit, we glimpse a hysterical dash towards the windows, where the courtiers risk their lives by jumping out. When the ceiling begins to collapse and the emperor begs for his life and those of his nobles, the rabbi tasks the golem with preventing the total destruction of the building. The fearless and stoic golem follows the rabbi's orders, bearing the weight of the gigantic beams, and saving the court from utter annihilation.

As directed by Rabbi Loew, the golem had been standing under one of the door pillars, replacing an armored guard who had left his station. Visually, even before the ceiling collapses, the golem functions as a protector of the court. While the gigantic Ahasverus, who threatens to emerge from the image, reaches the "beams of the ceiling," the immense golem holds up those same beams—which then break in half, forming a triangular shape around everyone present.[108] This shape transforms the seemingly static architecture of the court into a kind of tent, reminiscent of the makeshift abodes of Jews wandering in the desert.[109] It also resembles the angular homes in the ghetto, thereby undoing the sharp dichotomy between the wholeness and symmetry of the court and the asymmetrical, broken forms of the ghetto.

The story of Ahasverus first appeared in anti-Jewish propaganda: as characterized in a 1602 German chapbook, this man, once a cobbler, "refused to allow Jesus to rest on the wall of his house when he went by bearing his cross" and was thereupon punished with eternal wandering.[110] The Christian courtiers who laugh at Ahasverus are staring into a distorting mirror, their own antisemitic

The golem saves the court and the Jewish community.

biases exposed. The film makes this clear, as Cathy Gelbin observes, through high-angle shots that position viewers where the screen and Ahasverus would be, looking down at the mocking faces of the courtiers.[111] In this manner, those in power at the court are visually demoted, even ridiculed, whereas the supposedly powerless Jews can decide to bring ruin upon the court or else to save the courtiers. Rabbi Loew uses the cinematic medium in the court scene to save the lives of his people, reappropriating an antisemitic trope for his own purposes. He educates the hedonistic courtiers, showing them that the borders between myth and reality, between moving image and flesh-and-blood human, are not stable and can be manipulated. He enlists the golem—a fundamentally cinematic figure in its muteness and artificial doubling of human life—to teach the court and, by extension, the viewers of the film, a lesson in empathy.

When the ceiling of the court begins to collapse, we see pieces of it fall on those present, wounding and killing them. The chaos that erupts and the mad scrambling of the courtiers evoke, both emotionally and visually, the fear of war and bombardment. In the context of the recent war and its explosions, which caused trenches to collapse and bury their occupants, the court scene warns of the destructive effects of a lack of empathy toward others, specifically the imagined Jews on Rabbi Loew's projected screen and their Prague counterparts, the Jews in the ghetto. The golem embodies a savior fantasy that Wegener himself could not fulfill on the battlefield. While experiencing the helplessness of the courtiers and witnessing the casualties, Weimar spectators could also enjoy the rabbi's success.

But Wegener does more than turn the court into a battlefield in this scene; he also comments on the position of the Jewish population in the context of World War I and its aftermath. The courtiers' jeering of the exiled Jews echoes the rise of antisemitic sentiment during the war, when Germany's victory no longer appeared secure. Right-wing nationalists positioned Jews as a suspect group within the German nation, and the German military undertook a census in an effort to prove that they were dodging duty—although German Jews served loyally alongside other German citizens and suffered equal, if not greater, losses.[112] Rabbi Loew models a compassionate rather than vengeful approach in commanding the golem to rescue the very people who had just ordered the expulsion of the Jews and ridiculed their ancestors. Representing the Jews of Prague, Rabbi Loew saves the imperiled nation and its leaders, rather than stabbing them in the back, as Jews were accused of having done to the German nation during the war. While physically supporting the structure of the court, the golem figuratively holds up the image of German Jewry.

At the same time, as Nicholas Baer has shown, the image of the golem supporting the beams also resembles Dutch and German pictorial depictions of the biblical Samson as he grasps, and ultimately pulls down, the pillars of the Temple of Dagon in an act of self-destructive revenge. A powerful and manly alternative to the meek and effeminate diasporic Jew (such as the rabbi's assistant), the golem further represents, in this scene, the ideal of the Zionist "muscle Jew."[113] Likewise, the figure of Ahasverus, the wandering Jew, is reconfigured, in twentieth-century Zionist art and literature, into a Zionist allegory through its return to the Promised Land, as Todd Presner claims.[114] Associated via dissolve effects with the Star of David (as articulated above), a twentieth-century Zionist symbol, the golem becomes a muscular response to Ahasverus, the ridiculed, tormented Jew. The film ends, fittingly, with the near-destruction of the Jewish ghetto, symbol of an obsolete way of life, and with the golem's escape from the ghetto.

The Face of Things

In the final act of the film, the ghetto itself comes under attack, as the golem runs amok, setting the rabbi's home and the entire ghetto on fire. The film is tinted orange-red at this point, amplifying the sense of calamity. While the emperor has learned his lesson and annulled the edict of expulsion, societal order cannot be fully restored because of the illicit love affair occurring within the ghetto walls and under the rabbi's roof. Venturing into horror-genre territory, Wegener has the jealous assistant—reminiscent of Johann Wolfgang von Goethe's sorcerer's apprentice who cannot control his magical broom—resurrect the golem after its de-animation by the cautious rabbi. The golem then becomes an altered, uncontrollable menace. In this respect, the shell-shock atmosphere of the film carries over from the dangerous creation of the golem, through the court scene and the dead strewn all around, to the destruction of the rabbi's home and the ghetto itself.

Concomitantly, the golem's rampage is bracketed by tender scenes: first at court and then, at the very end, outside the ghetto's walls. The golem's physical act of rescue at court follows his emotional awakening earlier in the scene, when one of the women attending

The burning ghetto.

the festival hands him a rose to test his response. Earlier in the film, the nobleman Florian held a rose during his ghetto visit and gave it to Miriam. The romantic rose symbolizes court culture while also pointing to the possibility of romance across religious boundaries and even between a human and a clay anthropoid. It also links the 1920 film to the 1914/1915 adaptation, in which Wegener smells a rose bush while walking the streets of Hildesheim, his face softening as a result. A close-up on Wegener's face holding the rose up to his nose shows his rigid mouth begin to form a smile, suggesting a tempered longing. Wegener makes the point that the golem's heroic and even stoic behavior does not stem from a lack of ability to feel. Quite the contrary: it complements this monster's newfound desire and underscores the lack of empathy in the courtiers and their inability to consider the Jewish population as equally human.

The golem's expression softens as he smells the rose.

The Golem, How He Came into the World does not merely recreate the ruptures wrought by World War I or its shell-shock logic; it also suggests the potential for reinvesting life with meaning after the mass carnage of the war. In addition to the expressive architecture and the starry constellations, the final scenes of the film exhibit this potential. Only after being reanimated by the famulus for a vengeful purpose does the golem become dangerous and enraged, resembling Ahasverus in the court scene. It throws Florian off the tower of the rabbi's house and drags the unconscious Miriam out of her home and through the streets. Ultimately sparing her life, the golem breaks out of the ghetto walls, startling the children playing in the grass. The expressions of the children initially resemble the horrified, open-mouthed gazes of the courtiers when they first encounter the golem. But the mise-en-scène changes the overall atmosphere and affect of the moment. At court, the golem appeared immense and foreboding, but in relation to the gigantic ghetto walls, its stature is reduced. A long shot shows it standing in the middle of the field, forlorn. The open field also creates a counterpoint to the physiognomic aesthetic of ghetto architecture and the stylized setting of the court. This in-between space mitigates the extremes of ghetto and court, enabling a reciprocal encounter between the golem, as a Jewish creation, and the Christian world.

Just as the landscape looks more open and natural outside the ghetto walls—even though this scene, like the rest of the film, was shot in the studio—so the golem appears to enjoy the spontaneity of play, a departure from its usual role of obeying commands. In this final scene, the golem is no longer the living-dead automaton that carries out orders, or even the vengeful monster that has murdered

The golem ventures out of the ghetto on its own.

A smiling golem lifts the child in its arms.

Florian, but rather, it gains a new lease on life that ironically marks the end of its existence. A naïve child approaches the golem with an apple in her hand, symbolically tempting him into the human realm. The golem lifts the girl in its arms to better enjoy her proximity, and as the child fingers the golem's capsule, her unwitting curiosity brings its short-lived existence to a conclusion. By staging his last few moments as gentle and playful—even tender, in contrast to the previous bout of destructive rage—Wegener suggests that the golem's creation, the golem's "life," was not in vain. Balázs wrote in 1924:

> Every child knows that things have a face.... Children have no difficulty understanding these physiognomies. This is because they do not yet judge things purely as tools, means to an end, useful objects not to be dwelt on. They regard

each thing as an autonomous living being with a soul and face of its own. . . . No art is as well qualified to represent this "face of things" as film. For film presents not just a once-and-for-all rigid physiognomy, but a mysterious play of expressions.[115]

This final scene strikes the viewer because of its mutuality: from the creature's perspective, the child also appears as a wondrous phenomenon. The golem lifts her up in an all-too-human gesture that reminds the viewer of the golem's fundamental inhumanity. Sitting in its arms, the child, like the viewer, is now at eye level with the golem, almost equal to it. While Rabbi Loew attempted to end the golem's life after the monster had completed its mission and served the communal needs of the Jews, here the child de-animates the golem inadvertently. This "death" is affirmed in the film as a more fitting and harmonious one. "It is as if," writes Steve Choe, "the golem recognizes its own finitude as a living being," and the viewer understands that this monster is "not an invincible, monolithic machine, a weapon tasked with killing the other, but a vulnerable being."[116] Importantly, the child perceives the clay monster as a playmate rather than as a utilitarian object. Through the girl's gaze, the golem, no longer needed for carrying out the rabbi's orders or rescuing the court, momentarily attains an independent life. Because the child perceives the face of the golem, viewers too can suddenly experience the anthropoid less as an uncanny monster or machine than as a "living being with a soul and face of its own."

Significantly, this recognition takes place vis-à-vis the Christian child playing outside the ghetto, echoing the golem's encounter with the Christian woman in the court. Unlike the eternally wandering Jew, forever denied a resting place, the golem, a product of Jewish society, can be embraced by the Christian child and, implicitly, by the viewer. As the girl plays with the golem, we see a close-up of her fingers on the capsule, similar to the close-up of the rabbi's hands

The golem barely visible under the pile of children and flowers.

before he inserted the animating parchment. The film establishes, in this manner, a continuum between child and old man, Christian and Jew, just as it also reveals the humanity of the clay monster. When her fingers begin to withdraw the star-capsule, the golem does not stop her, however, as it attempted to do with the rabbi in a previous scene. It drops the girl and collapses to the ground, becoming an inanimate sculpture once more.

A moment later, the children gather and sit on this piece of clay, tossing the all-important capsule into the air as though it were a toy. The overabundance of flowers held by the children and strewn around the golem contrasts with the single rose that previously triggered the golem's emotional awakening. It evokes a kind of burial scene, the children unwittingly covering the inanimate being with memorial flowers. The film's final scene makes clear that Wegener sought not only to covertly re-create the atmosphere of World War I but also to point towards the path for recuperation: his golem can, for the first time in the narrative's history, make the choice of where, when, and how to end its brief existence.

At the end of the 1914/1915 film, the golem was cast from the tower and its body shattered to pieces, paving the way for Jewish integration into German society. In the finale of the 1920 film, by contrast, the golem figure remains intact, carried back into the ghetto on the shoulders of the Jewish crowd, perhaps to be reanimated at a future moment of great necessity.[117] The golem is honored at the end of its life, unlike the millions of young soldiers who died anonymous and futile deaths on the battlefields of World War I. But the significance of the golem's animation also derives from its ability to cross the threshold to the Christian world, embracing its innocent children, who allow us to forget, momentarily, the ill-intentioned court.

Awaking from the "haunting visions" of the film into "mundane existence," Hans Wollenberg, the Jewish editor of the widely distributed film magazine *Lichtbild-Bühne*, wrote that after the film, he looked around and saw "every well-known person in art- and film-Berlin." The hearts of those present at the screening rejoiced in "triumphant knowledge": "In the competition of nations over the flickering art of film," Wollenberg contends, "this time the blue ribbon is ours."[118] Wollenberg found in the golem's worthwhile mission on the screen an occasion for national victory, in which he himself could partake: the third Golem film was received as the hero of the day.[119] Purportedly, Germany could achieve this postwar victory through an embrace of Jewish motifs and the recruitment of Jewish artists, actors, and writers—including actor Ernst Deutsch, cinematographer Freund, and score composer Hans Landsberger. As a clay monster molded and animated, the golem figure aptly served Wegener and his audiences as a mythic benchmark for the development of film, combining Jewish and non-Jewish aspirations under the unified banner of German cinema's technological magic. Even while the film implicitly promoted Zionist ideals, the last shot superimposing the Star of David on the ghetto, its ultimate success relied on the integration of Jews into the German film industry.

Epilogue: The Afterlives of *The Golem, How He Came into the World*

With the release of the 1920 film, the golem had fulfilled Wegener's ethical and aesthetic purposes, and the director never returned to the golem story or embodied this figure again. His incarnation of the golem left an indelible mark on twentieth-century culture, however, both through film screenings in the United States and through a long-lasting visual legacy in film, comics, and theater. Wegener's 1920 film had its US premiere on June 19, 1921, under the title *The Golem*, at the nine-hundred-seat Criterion Theater near Times Square. In October, amidst a lengthy run of close to seventeen weeks of consecutive screenings, the *New York Times* reported that "the golem is going and going."[120] Rather than using Landsberger's modern symphonic score, the Criterion Theater arranged its own music for the film, drawing on popular Jewish opera and cinema hits like Jacob Sandler's "Eli, Eli." It also framed the film through a theatrical prologue depicting the 1499 expulsion of the Jewish community from Nuremberg, striving to connect the plot of the fantastic film to past historical events, as well as to the present. Since the film screened in the aftermath of the May 1921 quotas placed on immigration to the United States, Jewish viewers, distressed by the plight of Jewish refugees in Eastern Europe, considered the golem narrative a timely one. One critic even hoped that, in response to these current events, "someone would fashion another Golem and place upon him the words that would make him act."[121]

In December of 1921, a Yiddish-language operetta, *Der goylem* (*The Golem*), including a sixty-person choir and thirty musical numbers, premiered in New York. Taking a more light-hearted approach, the operetta nonetheless conjured up scenes of Jewish homelessness and wandering, evoking the present-day difficulties that Jewish refugees were facing.[122] Max Gabel, producer and star of the operetta, drew heavily on the visual language of Wegener's 1920 film: his Rabbi Loew discovers the animating word "truth" (*emes*, in Yiddish) when it is projected on the walls of his house (with fire spurting out of the letters); he then traces the word onto a piece of parchment. The Yiddish-speaking rabbi places this parchment in a hexagram, a Star of David, a more explicitly Jewish symbol than the five-pointed metal capsule of Wegener's film.[123]

Photos of Max Gabel dressed as the golem reveal that he directly copied Wegener's costume. Gabel's attire included a headdress (although not made of the same sculpted clay), large boots, a thick belt, and ropes tied around his arms.[124] Just as Wegener had employed his partner Lyda Salmonova in the role of Miriam, Rabbi Loew's "modest" daughter, Gabel also engaged his wife and onstage partner, the popular melodrama actress Jenny Goldstein, in that role. In multiple ads and photos, Goldstein appeared with long, braided hair and an Oriental costume and jewelry, reminiscent of Salmonova's costume in the film.[125] The golem's desire for Miriam awakens and intensifies throughout the operetta, as it does in the film, and the couple's extra-theatrical relationship enhanced the erotic dimension of this love interest.

Gabel's operetta was the first of many productions across theater, opera, cinema, and the fine arts that have stood in explicit or implicit dialogue with Wegener's iconic portrayal of the golem on the silver screen. Eugene d'Albert's 1926 opera drew inspiration, as Benjamin Goose has shown, both from the costumes of the 1920 film and from its central scene, in which Rabbi Loew projects the images of Jewish ancestors on the court wall.[126] Subsequent golem films, such as Julien Duviver's 1936 French-Czech co-production *Le Golem*, did not adopt Wegener's aesthetic approach but nonetheless dealt with

Yiddish theater actor Max Gabel in a costume replicating Wegener's cinematic golem.

themes that echoed the German film, such as the hardship inflicted upon a Jewish community by a tyrannical emperor. In James Whale's 1931 *Frankenstein* film, the monster created by Dr. Frankenstein encounters a little girl who hands him a flower, reminiscent of the child at the end of *The Golem, How Came into the World*. This gesture moves the monster to smile, as Wegener did when enacting the golem, but he soon returns to his monstrous role, violently throwing the child into the water and drowning her.[127]

Twenty-first-century American animation and comics continues to explicitly recall Wegener's golem, replicating both the costume of the clay giant, as designed by Belling, and some of the narrative elements of the Weimar film. To take two prominent examples, in a 2006 episode of *The Simpsons*, Bart Simpson animates a clay golem (voiced by Richard Lewis) that looks almost exactly like Paul Wegener's golem. As in Max Gabel's case, *The Simpsons'* creators ironically mark the golem as Jewish through the Star of David on its chest, its use of "Jewish humor," and its ultimate marriage to a feminine playdough giant, a ceremony performed by a rabbi under a traditional Jewish ḥuppah.[128] In James Sturm's 2001 graphic narrative *The Golem's Mighty Swing*, a traveling Jewish barnstorming team in the 1920s dresses its only African American player in the costume worn by Wegener in the film, claiming that the costume came "all the way from Germany."[129] The use of the costume fuels the flames of antisemitic resentment in the small Midwestern towns where the team plays, culminating in a violent rampage during which the single African American ballplayer saves his Jewish teammates.

No other golem film or artwork has shaped the *image* of the clay monster in modern popular culture, at least visually, to the extent of *The Golem, How He Came into the World*. Wegener did not shy away, moreover, from the horrors of the golem narrative, depicting it in the context of Christian-Jewish conflict, as well as the ghetto's destruction and the murder of the courtier Florian. His third golem film enabled later artists to tap into these violent and often-repressed motifs of the golem narrative, to draw on them for their own cultural and political agendas. While the *Simpsons* episode uses and mocks stereotypes about New York Jews (particularly through the voice of comedienne Fran Drescher), *The Golem's Mighty Swing* explores how racist treatment of both Jews and African Americans renders them monstrous others.

The representation of the golem's "purely visual existence" as a cinematically animated figure takes place, in *The Golem, How*

He Came into the World, within an expressive, sculptural mise-en-scène, vivified through lighting and cinematography. The forces of animation in the film outbalance those of destruction, allowing the golem to emerge from its predetermined function as mechanized savior-protector and reveal the extent of its fury and fragility. The film thus provides a visual record of the aftermath of World War I, projecting a Jewish community magically forging new weapons in its dugouts and turning the Prague court into a battle scene. We can locate the urgency and endurance of *The Golem* in this employment of the horror-gothic genre to comment on the monstrosity of war and the ethical peril facing the German nation. With the 1920 production, a golem had truly come into the world, inviting ongoing forms of citation and conversation, and inhabiting the popular imagination for a long time to come.

CREDITS

Director:
Paul Wegener
Carl Boese

Writers:
Paul Wegener
Henrik Galeen
Production Company:
Projektions-AG-Union (PAGU) Berlin

Distributor:
Universum film (UFA)

Produced by:
Paul Davidson

Cast:
Paul Wegener (Golem)
Albert Steinrück (Rabbi Loew)
Lyda Salmonova (Rabbi Loew's
    daughter, Miriam)
Ernst Deutsch (Famulus, Rabbi's assistant)
Otto Gebühr (Kaiser Rudolph II)
Lothar Müthel (Nobleman Florian)
Loni Nest (Young girl)
Hans Sturm (Jewish elder)
Greta Schröder (Woman with rose at court)

Music:
Hans Landsberger

Cinematography:
Karl Freund
Guido Seeber

Production Design:
Hans Poelzig
Kurt Richter

Costume Design:
Rochus Gliese

Runtime:
84 minutes

Sound Mix:
No sound

Color:
Shot in black and white; color tinting added.

Aspect Ratio:
1.33:1

Film Length:
1,954 m

Negative Format:
35 mm

Cinematographic Process:
Spherical

Printed Film Format:
35 mm

Release Dates:
October 29, 1920 (Germany);
    June 19, 1921 (USA)

NOTES

1 *Der Golem, wie er in die Welt kam*, Paul Wegener and Carl Boese (Germany: Universum Film AG, 1920). This film has long been available in DVD in multiple versions (such as Transit Classics, 2004). In 2018, the Royal Film Archive of Belgium–Cinematek and the F. W. Murnau Foundation supervised a 4k digital restoration of the film, based on the original negative: *Der Golem, wie er in die Welt kam* (Universum Film GmbH, 2019). All of the screen shots included in this book have been taken from the 2019 restored version.

2 For accounts of Paul Wegener's theatrical career, see Heide Schönemann, *Paul Wegener: Frühe Moderne im Film* (Stuttgart and London: Menges, 2003), 9–13.

3 Katharina Loew, "The Spirit of Technology: Early German Thinking about Film," *New German Critique* 41, no. 2 (2014): 126.

4 Paul Wegener, "On the Artistic Possibilities of the Motion Picture," in *The Promise of Cinema: German Film Theory, 1907–1933*, ed. Anton Kaes, Nicholas Baer, and Michael Cowan (Oakland: University of California Press, 2016), 207.

5 *The Student of Prague* premiered in August of 1913 and by December of 1913 Wegener noted in his repertoire book that he had completed the screenplay for his next film, *The Golem*. "Repertoirebuch 1895–1924," Nachlass Paul Wegener: Sammlung Kai Möller, Deutsches Filminstitut, Frankfurt am Main.

6 Thomas Elsaesser calls this phenomenon the "Wegener combination of romanticism and technology" and considers postwar German expressionist cinema to be the "tail-end of this first truce between highbrow culture and a lowbrow medium [i.e., film]," rather than a new development. Thomas Elsaesser, *Weimar Cinema and After: Germany's Historical Imaginary* (London: Routledge, 2000), 65. See also Katherine Loew's discussion of how fairy tales "appealed to often-latent desires for a 'new mythology' and offered economic, ideological, and creative advantages," becoming acceptable for cinematic representation even "among the most culturally conservative critics." Loew, "Spirit of Technology," 134.

7 Anton Kaes, *Shell Shock Cinema: Weimar Culture and the Wounds of War* (Princeton, NJ: Princeton University Press, 2009), 57.

8 Paul Wegener, "Der Golem und die Tänzerin," 4.4-80/18.3, Schriftgutarchiv, Stiftung Deutsche Kinemathek, Filmmuseum Berlin; all translations are mine unless otherwise noted.

9 This golem film, wrote one critic, "is a milestone in the history of film art because it establishes new relationships to modern art." Another critic remarked that "cinema has begun to have its own literary history, like stage drama, with new excavations and adaptations," like Wegener's third golem film, his "Ur-Golem." See Eugen Tannenbaum, "Der Golem, wie er in die Welt kam (B. Z. am Mittag, no. 203)," *Kritiken über das Film-werk: Der Golem, Wie er in die Welt kam*, Schriftgutarchiv, Stiftung Deutsche Kinema-thek, Filmmuseum Berlin, 3; A. F., "Der Golem, wie er in die Welt kam," *Der Film* no. 44, October 30, 1920, 30.

10 Paul Wegener, "Mein Werdegang," in *Paul Wegener: Sein Leben und Seine Rollen; Ein Buch von ihm und über ihn*, ed. Kai Möller (Hamburg: Rowohlt, 1954), 35.

11 The *Berliner Börsen-Courier*, for example, reported prominently in September 1915 on Wegener's first post-service acting role, commending his Iron Cross. "Schauspielkunst und Krieg," *Berliner Börsen-Courier*, September 1, 1915.

12 The 1920 production arrested viewers with its "images of unheard of beauty and with its twisting and flourishing lines." A. F., "Der Golem, wie er in die Welt kam," 30.

13 Edan Dekel and David Gantt Gurley, "How the Golem Came to Prague," *Jewish Quarterly Review* 103, no. 2 (2013): 242–43, 251.

14 Cathy Gelbin, *The Golem Returns: From German Romantic Literature to Global Jewish Culture, 1808–2008* (Ann Arbor: The University of Michigan Press, 2011), 13.

15 Dekel and Gurley, "How the Golem Came to Prague," 251.

16 Paul Wegener, "Warum ich für den Film spiele," Nachlass Paul Wegener: Sammlung Kai Möller, Deutsches Filminstitut, Frankfurt am Main, 2.

17 Gustav Meyrink, *The Golem*, trans. Madge Pemberton (New York: Dover, 1986), 15-16.

18 Holitscher sued Wegener on the grounds of plagiarism, although it remains unclear, according to Sigrid Mayer, which of the three films served as the basis for this suit. Sigrid Mayer, *Golem: Die literarische Rezeption eines Stoffes* (Bern: Herbert Lang, 1975), 154 n. 8.

19 Oded Shai, "Fantazia, folklor, agada, ve-erotika: sippurei ha-"golem" ba-sifrut ha-germanit be-reshit ha-me'a ha-'esrim," *Tabur* 4 (2010): 83.

20 Arthur Holitscher, *Der Golem: Ghettolegende in drei Aufzügen* (Berlin: Fischer Verlag, 1908), 125.

21 Shai, "Fantazia, folklor, agada, ve-erotika," 83.

22 Paul Wegener and Henrik Galeen, "Der Golem: Phantastisches Filmspiel in vier Akten," in *Henrik Galeen: Film—Materialien*, ed. Hans-Michael Bock and Wolfgang Jacobson (Hamburg: Cinegraph, 1992), 3–4.

23 An assimilated Jew from a small town in Eastern Galicia, Henrik Galeen had assisted Max Reinhart in Berlin and worked in Swiss theaters prior to embarking on a successful film career as screenwriter, director, and occasional actor. In addition to directing the popular *Alraune* (1927), Galeen wrote the scripts for *Nosferatu* (F. W. Murnau, 1921) and *Waxworks* (Paul Leni, 1923). For a discussion of Galeen's career and his film Alraune, see Ofer Ashkenazi, *Weimar Film and Modern Jewish Identity* (New York: Palgrave Macmillan, 2012), 84–85.

24 Part of the chase scene and the ending of the 1914/1915 film, including the reconciliatory embrace, have been found and restored: *Fragment des Spielfilms Der Golem: Phantastisches Spiel in vier Akten*, Paul Wegener and Henrik Galeen (1915; Germany: absolut MEDIEN, 2007), DVD.

25 The influential *Autorenfilm* (author-film) *The Student of Prague* re-created Prague's old Jewish cemetery for one of its scenes, as the Jewish community did not allow filming in

the actual cemetery. Lotte H. Eisner, *The Haunted Screen: Expressionism in the German Cinema and the Influence of Max Reinhardt*, trans. Roger Greaves (Berkeley: University of California Press, 2008), 42.

26 Wegener and Galeen, "Der Golem," 5.

27 Wegener and Galeen, "Der Golem," 5.

28 Schönemann, *Paul Wegener*, 78.

29 Paul Wegener, *Der Golem, wie er in die Welt kam: Eine Geschichte in fünf Kapiteln* (Berlin: August Scherl GmbH, 1921), 9. See also Rosenfeld's 1934 discussion of Wegener's facial features and costume: Beate Rosenfeld, *Die Golemsage und ihre Verwertung in der deutschen Literatur* (Breslau: Dr. Hans Priebatsch, 1934), 147.

30 Andrej, "Der Golem wie er in die Welt kam: Ufa-Palast am Zoo," *Film-Kurier*, no. 245, October 30, 1920, 1.

31 A. F. "Der Golem, wie er in die Welt kam," 30.

32 Wegener, "Artistic Possibilities," 207.

33 Georg Lukács, "Thoughts Toward an Aesthetic of the Cinema," in *The Promise of Cinema: German Film Theory 1907–1933*, ed. Anton Kaes, Nicholas Baer, and Michael Cowan (Berkeley: University of California Press, 2016), 378.

34 Lukács, "Thoughts Toward an Aesthetic of the Cinema," 378.

35 Lukács, "Thoughts Toward an Aesthetic of the Cinema," 379-380.

36 Wegener and Galeen, "Der Golem," 12–13.

37 Arnold Zweig, "Der Golem," *Die Schaubühne*, no. 10, March 11, 1915, 226.

38 Zweig, "Der Golem," 226–27. Adolf Behne also viewed this scene as one of the aesthetic high points both in Wegener's acting career and in this particular film. See Adolf Behne, "Der Golem," *Bild und Film*, no. 7/8 (1914/1915), 157. The screenplay directions run: "Golem als Silhouette gegen den Himmel. Breitet die Arme aus und guckt zu den Sternen empor." Wegener and Galeen, "Der Golem," 13.

39 Wegener and Galeen, "Der Golem," 8.

40 Wegener and Galeen, "Der Golem," 11.

41 Lukács, "Thoughts Toward an Aesthetic of the Cinema," 378, 380.

42 Behne, "Der Golem," 156.

43 Paul Wegener, "Die künstlerischen Möglichkeiten des Films," in *Paul Wegener: Sein Leben und seine Rollen: Ein Buch von ihm und über ihn*, ed. Kai Möller (Hamburg: Rowohlt, 1954), 111.

44 "Die künstlerischen Möglichkeiten des Films," 111.

45 Andrej, "Der Golem wie er in die Welt kam," 1.

46 The intertitles for *Der Golem, wie er in die Welt kam* in all the surviving versions can be found in Elfriede Ledig, *Paul Wegeners Golem-Filme im Kontext fantastischer Literatur:*

Grundfragen zur Gattungsproblematik fantastischen Erzählens (Munich: Verlaggemeinschaft Schaudig/Bauer/Ledig, 1989), 110, 116, 122.

47 Frances Guerin, *A Culture of Light: Cinema and Technology in 1920s Germany* (Minneapolis: University of Minnesota Press, 2005), 126.

48 Noa Steimatsky, *The Face on Film* (New York: Oxford University Press, 2017), 28.

49 Béla Balázs, *Béla Balázs: Early Film Theory*, ed. Erica Carter, trans. Rodney Livingstone (New York: Berghahn Books, 2010), 100.

50 Balázs, *Early Film Theory*, 101.

51 The five-pointed star, or pentagram, had a similar magical use and was often found on amulets alongside or interchanged with the hexagram. See Gershom Scholem, "The Star of David: History of a Symbol," in *The Messianic Idea in Judaism and Other Essays on Jewish Spirituality* (New York: Schocken Books, 1995), 259–64.

52 Kerry Wallach, *Passing Illusions: Jewish Visibility in Weimar Germany* (Ann Arbor: University of Michigan Press, 2017), 35.

53 According to Thomas Elsaesser, Expressionism was not a fixed style but *a way of stylizing* German cinema into a respectable art form that could technically "simulate stylistic authenticity, organic coherence and formal adequacy." Elsaesser, *Weimar Cinema and After*, 39.

54 Dietrich Scheunemann, "Activating the Differences: Expressionist Film and Early Weimar Cinema," in *Expressionist Film: New Perspectives*, ed. Dietrich Scheunemann (Rochester: Camden House, 2003), 19–20. See also Eisner, *The Haunted Screen*, 58–59.

55 Kaes, *Shell Shock Cinema*, 85–86.

56 Tannenbaum, "Der Golem, wie er in die Welt kam," 3.

57 "Medieval Ghetto in the Center Of Action in 'Golem' Film," *New York Tribune*, June 19, 1921, 2.

58 Herbert Ihering, "Der Schauspieler im Film," *Von Reinhardt bis Brecht: Vier jahrzehnte Theater und Film, vol. 1 1908–1923*, 380.

59 According to Wolffgang Fischer, Wegener's budget for the film was no less than five million German marks, an enormous sum for the postwar period. Wolffgang Fischer, "Der Golem, wie er in die Welt kam (Neue Zeit)," *Kritiken über das Filmwerk: Der Golem, Wie er in die Welt kam*, Schriftgutarchiv, Stiftung Deutsche Kinemathek, Filmmuseum Berlin, 8.

60 Claudia Dillmann, "Die Wirkung der Architektur ist eine magische: Hans Poelzig und der Film," in *Hans Poelzig: Bauten für den Film*, ed. Hans-Peter Reichmann, *Kinematograph* 12 (special issue) (Frankfurt am Main: Deutsches Filmmuseum, 1997), 26.

61 Dillmann, "Hans Poelzig und der Film," 28.

62 Dillmann, "Hans Poelzig und der Film," 33.

63 Dillmann, "Hans Poelzig und der Film," 28–29, 43.

64 Spyros Papapetros maintains that the set design exhibits "a material convergence between living bodies and architectural environments." *On the Animation of the Inorganic: Art, Architecture, and the Extension of Life* (Chicago: University of Chicago Press, 2012), 224.

65 One critic even complained that in *The Golem* "nature receives such blows in the ribs that it realizes the unreal." Eduard Korrodi, "Golem—Wegener—Poelzig," in *Kein Tag ohne Kino: Schriftsteller über den Stummfilm*, ed. Fritz Güttinger (Frankfurt am Main: Deutsches Filmmuseum, 1984), 325.

66 Paul Westheim, "Eine Filmstadt von Poelzig," *Das Kunstblatt* 4, no. 11 (1920): 331–32.

67 "The Screen," *The New York Times*, June 20, 1921, 20.

68 Heinrich de Fries, "Raumgestaltung im Film," *Wasmuths Monatshefte für Baukunst*, no. 5 (1920–21): 81. For further testimony of Poelzig's use of the term "mauscheln," see his biography: Theodor Heuss, *Hans Poelzig: Das Lebensbild eines deutschen Baumeisters* (Tübingen: Verlag Ernst Wasmuth, 1948), 69–70.

69 Meyrink, *The Golem*, 16–17. Unlike Meyrink's depiction of the ghetto as potentially "hostile" or "malicious," the American reviews of Wegener's film interpreted the ghetto homes more positively, viewing them as leaning "affectionately against each other." "Reinhardt's Art on Screen to Be Seen Soon on Broadway," *New York Tribune*, April 10, 1921, 4.

70 Herman G. Scheffauer, "The Vivifying Space," in *Introduction to the Art of Movies*, ed. Lewis Jacobs (New York: Noonday Press, 1960), 84. See also Noah Isenberg, "Of Monsters and Magicians: Paul Wegener's *The Golem: How He Came into the World* (1920)," in *Weimar Cinema: An Essential Guide to Classic Films of the Era*, ed. Noah Isenberg (New York: Columbia University Press, 2009), 46–48.

71 Fries, "Raumgestaltung im Film," 81.

72 Isenberg, "Of Monsters and Magicians," 47–48.

73 Andrej, "Der Golem wie er in die Welt kam," 1.

74 Paul Wegener and Andrej, "Ein Gespräch mit Paul Wegener: Einführendes zum 'Golem'," *Film-Kurier*, no. 244, October 29, 1920, 2.

75 Valerie Weinstein, "Anti-Semitism or Jewish 'Camp'? Ernst Lubitsch's *Schuhpalast Pinkus* (1916) and *Meyer aus Berlin* (1918)," *German Life and Letters* 59, no. 1 (2006): 506.

76 Cynthia Walk, "Romeo with Sidelocks: Jewish-Gentile Romance in E. A. Dupont's *Das alte Gesetz* (1923) and Other Early Weimar Assimilation Films," in *The Many Faces of Weimar Cinema: Rediscovering Germany's Filmic Legacy*, ed. Christian Rogowski (Rochester, NY: Camden House, 2010), 91.

77 Miriam's ultimate punishment, through the golem's murder of Florian, "reinstate[s] the patriarchal order and its ethnic-religious boundaries." Gelbin, *The Golem Returns*, 120–21.

78 Wallach, *Passing Illusions*, 28.

79 M. W., "Erstaufführung des neuen Wegenerfilms in den U.-T.-Theatern," *Deutscher Kurier* no. 16, January 15, 1915.

80 Rosenfeld, *Die Golemsage*, 137; Tannenbaum, "Der Golem, wie er in die Welt kam," 3.

81 Carl Boese, "Erinnerungen an die Entstehung und an die Aufnahmen eines der berühmtesten Stummfilme: Der Golem," Sammlung *Der Golem, Wie er in die Welt kam*, Schriftgutarchiv, Stiftung Deutsche Kinemathek, Filmmuseum Berlin, 2.

82 Daniel Wildmann, "Desire, Excess, and Integration: Orientalist Fantasies, Moral Sentiments, and the Place of Jews in German Society as Portrayed in Films of the Weimar Republic," in *Orientalism, Gender, and the Jews: Literary and Artistic Transformations of European National Discourses*, ed. Ulrike Brunotte, Anna-Dorothea Ludewig, and Axel Stähler (Berlin: Walter de Gruyter, 2014), 144.

83 See Ulrich Johannes Beil, "Medialität und Auratisierung: Zur Magie der Schrift in Paul Wegeners *Der Golem, wie er in die Welt kam*," *Internationales Archiv für Sozialgeschichte der deutschen Literatur* 42, no. 2 (2017): 515–20.

84 Eliphas Levi, *Transcendental Magic: Its Doctrine and Ritual*, trans. Arthur Edward Waite (Boston: Weiser Books, 2001), 237, 239.

85 Boese, "Erinnerungen an die Entstehung," 13.

86 Wegener, "Mein Werdegang," 35.

87 Letter to Ernst Pietsch, December 2, 1914, Nachlass Paul Wegener: Sammlung Kai Möller, Deutsches Filminstitut, Frankfurt am Main.

88 Stephen Bull, "No Man's Land," International Encyclopedia of the First World War, August 20, 2015, https://encyclopedia.1914-1918-online.net/article/no_mans_land.

89 Wegener wrote his original Flanders diary within the pages of his soldier's identification and pay book. In 1933 he published an expanded version of these notes. Paul Wegener, "Flandrisches Tagebuch," October 31, 1914 and December 1, 1915, Nachlass Paul Wegener: Sammlung Kai Möller, Deutsches Filminstitut, Frankfurt am Main.

90 Wegener, *Flandrisches Tagebuch 1914* (Berlin: Rowohlt, 1933), 56.

91 Wegener, *Flandrisches Tagebuch 1914*, 143.

92 Wegener, *Flandrisches Tagebuch 1914*, 145.

93 Wegener, Letter to Pietsch, December 9, 1914, Nachlass Paul Wegener: Sammlung Kai Möller, Deutsches Filminstitut, Frankfurt am Main.

94 Wegener, Letter to Pietsch, December 12, 1914, Nachlass Wegener: Sammlung Kai Möller, Deutsches Filminstitut; *Flandrisches Tagebuch 1914*, 147.

95 Wegener, Letter to Pietsch, January 8, 1915, Nachlass Wegener: Sammlung Kai Möller, Deutsches Filminstitut.

96 Wegener, Letter to Pietsch, February 20, 1915, Nachlass Wegener: Sammlung Kai Möller, Deutsches Filminstitut.

97 Paul Wegener, "Schauspielerei und Film," *Berliner Tageblatt* no. 27, January 15, 1915.

98 According to the *Breslauer Zeitung* critic, the screening of the *Golem* film had an "especially timely appeal" owing to the "heroic glory" of its creator, lieutenant Paul Wegener,

an actor who had advanced from "hero of the theater" to "hero of the battlefront."
"Berliner Theater," *Breslauer Zeitung*, January 19, 1915.

99 Korrodi, "Golem—Wegener—Poelzig," 322.

100 Wegener, "Flandrisches Tagebuch," October 31, 1914, Nachlass Paul Wegener:
Sammlung Kai Möller, Deutsches Filminstitut, Frankfurt am Main.

101 Kaes, *Shell Shock Cinema*, 3–4.

102 Kaes, *Shell Shock Cinema*, 4.

103 Susanne Holl and Friedrich Kittler, "Ablösen des Streifens vom Buche: Eine Allegorese
von Wegeners drei Golemfilmen," *Blickführung*, no. 41 (1996): 107, 109.

104 Holl and Friedrich Kittler, "Ablösen des Streifens," 106.

105 Wegener, *Flandrisches Tagebuch 1914*, 188. Wegener also writes about the "useless attacks
against machine guns, the entanglement of trenches, canals, and barbed wire, without
sufficient artillery preparation." *Flandrisches Tagebuch 1914*, 159.

106 In the 1847 tale, when the emperor can no longer hold back his laughter, the ceiling
begins to sink, only to be arrested by the rabbi himself rather than by a golem. Ludwig
Weisel's narrative is translated in Hillel J. Kieval, "Pursuing the Golem of Prague: Jewish
Culture and the Invention of a Tradition," *Modern Judaism* 17, no. 1 (1997): 11. See also
Leopold Weisel, "Sagen der Prager Juden," in *Sippurim: Eine Sammlung jüdischer Volks-
sagen, Erzählungen, Mythen, Chroniken, Denkwürdigkeiten*, ed. Wolf Pascheles (Prague:
Wolf Pascheles, 1858), 52.

107 Isenberg, "Of Monsters and Magicians," 41.

108 Wegener, *Der Golem, wie er in die Welt kam*, 50.

109 ". . . und die Decke senkte sich nur an den Seiten noch ein wenig wie das Dach eines
Zeltes," Wegener, *Der Golem, wie er in die Welt kam*, 52.

110 Galit Hasan-Rokem, "The Cobbler of Jerusalem in Finnish Folklore," in *The Wandering
Jew: Essays in Interpretation of a Christian Legend*, ed. Galit Hasan-Rokem and Alan
Dundes (Bloomington: Indiana University Press, 1986), 120.

111 Gelbin, *The Golem Returns*, 120.

112 "In October 1916, the German High Command and the Prussian war minister
commissioned a *Judenzählung*, or Jewish census, in order to obtain statistical evidence
that Jews were in fact disproportionately shirking military duty. . . . The very taking of
the census insinuated that German Jews were first and foremost *Jews* who had to be
excluded because they threatened the German nation." Kaes, *Shell Shock Cinema*, 111.
See also Tim Grady, *The German-Jewish Soldiers of the First World War in History and
Memory* (Liverpool: Liverpool University Press, 2011).

113 Nicholas Baer, "Messianic Musclemen: *Homunculus* (1916) and *Der Golem* (1920) as
Zionist Allegories," in *The Place of Politics in German Film*, ed. Martin Blumenthal-Barby
(Bielefeld: Aisthesis Verlag, 2014), 40–42.

114 Todd Samuel Presner, *Muscular Judaism: The Jewish Body and the Politics of Regeneration* (London: Routledge, 2007), 79–81.

115 Balázs, *Early Film Theory*, 46.

116 Steve Choe, *Afterlives: Allegories of Film and Mortality in Early Weimar Germany* (New York: Bloomsbury, 2014), 169, 173. Reading the film through the lens of Martin Buber's "I-Thou" philosophy, Choe contends that the ending enacts an "ethical relationship between human and technology," recognizing the "ontological strangeness" of the golem and ceasing to appropriate and exploit this figure (173).

117 In Reinhardt's 1909 theatrical production of *Hamlet*, in which Wegener played King Claudius, the dead Hamlet was carried at the end of the play above the heads of his comrades, his body stiff and arched. See Schönemann, *Paul Wegener*, 102.

118 Hans Wollenberg, "Der Golem," *Lichtbild-Bühne*, no. 44, October 30, 1920, 26.

119 Another film critic wrote: "Between Wegener's 'Golem' from before the war and the great feature film that is now being screened in the Berlin Ufa Palace, lies almost a decade of heaven-storming artistic and technical cinematic development. The small film industry has become a great power." "Der neue Wegener-Film," *Deutsche Lichtspiel-Zeitung*, no. 45, November 6, 1920, 4.

120 "Picture Plays and People," *The New York Times*, October 9, 1921, 4.

121 I. L. Bril, "The Golem," *Yidishes tageblat*, July 31, 1921, 12.

122 Albert Kövessy and Max Gabel, "Der goylem: muzikalishe legende in 3 akten un 4 tabloyen mit a prolog," 1921, The Lawrence Marwick Collection of Copyrighted Yiddish Plays, D 59524, Library of Congress, 5–6.

123 Kövessy and Gabel, "Der goylem," 11.

124 The *Variety* reviewer noted that "Max Gabel personating the legendary titular character is made up much like the screen image." Abel, "The Golem (in Yiddish)," *Variety*, no. 11, February 3, 1922, 18.

125 See Maks Gebil, "Maks Gebil dankt dem groyse oylem un der prese," *Forverts*, January 14, 1922, 4.

126 Benjamin Goose, "The Opera of the Film? Eugen d'Albert's *Der Golem*," *Cambridge Opera Journal* 19, no. 2 (2007): 144–45, 156–57.

127 *Frankenstein*, James Whale (1931; Universal Pictures, 1999), DVD.

128 *The Simpsons*, 4, "Treehouse of Horror XVII," David Silverman and Matthew C. Faughnan, Peter Gaffney, November 5, 2006, Fox Network.

129 James Sturm, *The Golem's Mighty Swing* (Montreal: Drawn and Quarterly, 2001), 29.